To: Connie & Bill – with
love and best regards.
l/C Balfaurun, Dec. 3, 2012

The Eagle Soars
John's Search For the Infinite

R.C. Balfour III

© 2013
by
R.C. Balfour III

ISBN: 978-1-935802-14-3

Cover design by Kevin McMillan

**FATHER
&
SON**
PUBLISHING, INC.
4909 N. Monroe Street
Tallahassee, Florida 32303-7015
www.fatherson.com
800-741-2712

Seek and ye shall find... and ye shall know the truth and the truth shall make you free.

(Luke 11:9b... John 8:3)

Table of Contents

Part III John and the Spirit

Dedication

I dedicate this book to my editors: my wife Virginia, my daughter Deborah, and my priest, the Rev. Jim Hobby who all worked tirelessly to produce a presentable manuscript.

Other Books by R.C. Balfour III

In Search Of TheAucilla

Fishing For The Abundant Life

He Turned The World Upside Down

Paul Speaks To Us Today

PREFACE

When I began thinking of writing a novel about the Apostle John, I discovered I had two things in common with the disciple. We were both avid fishermen, and we shared a desire to search for the Infinite—for the real meaning of life and where it was leading. This made writing the story much easier.

There are a multitude of legends about John, but I have used very few. Instead, I have drawn much of the story from scripture, principally the Gospel Of John. Essential to the story is the assumption that the beloved disciple is actually John, himself, as is the (unnamed) disciple in the episode about John the Baptist. In addition, I used some "spiritual imagination" or rather relied upon the leading of the Spirit.

I have used a number of Old and New Testament quotations and have italicized these passages; they are identified in the back of the book. Other New Testament segments are for the most part paraphrased as part of the story.

Scholarship is divided over the location of the Baptist's initial preaching and baptizing. Some early writers such as Origen and Eusebius claimed that the location was Bethabara, a small town just north of the Dead Sea on the *west* bank of the

Jordan. This town was still known at the time of Origen whereas Bethany across the Jordan had vanished. On the other hand, almost all of the earliest texts of John's gospel read "Bethany across the Jordan," (on the *east* bank). It is possible that this small village site was lost during the years, especially since the path of the river has changed. I have chosen Bethany on the east bank as I believe it to be most compatible with the early texts and with the narrative. It is, of course, not to be confused with Bethany near Jerusalem, the home of Lazarus.

Descriptions of the destruction of Jerusalem can be found in the writings of Josephus. The story of Domitian is based on *The Life of Domitian* by Suetonius as published in the Loeb Classical Library, 1914. The narrative of John's reclaiming the young bandit is based on a story in *The History of the Church* by Eusebius. The existence of the Roman penal colony on Patmos is well attested by Irenaeus, Clement of Alexandria, and Tacitus, all ancient writers. Other authors I read before writing the novel include Beth Moore, John MacArthur, Jerry B. Jenkins, Ellen Gunderson Traylor, John Robinson, James Byers, John Stott, Alan Culpepper, Barbara Green, Everett Aaron Edwards, Rodney A. Whitacre, and Mendel Nun. Also I feel I should mention the New Revised Standard Version of the Holy Bible. Its language is very clear and particularly meaningful to me.

R.C. Balfour III

PART I

John And The Baptist

I

Youth

The first winter winds blew over the sea, chilling its waters. Responding to the season, schools of musht were forming and swimming closer to shore as they had done for a thousand years.

Just before day a lone figure waded out from shore. He was dressed in a simple loin cloth with the folds of a cast net gathered in his arms. As he moved deeper into the sea, his eyes searched diligently for any movement in the water. Suddenly there they were, a dozen or more musht swimming on a path toward him. At the right moment, with his hand gripping the edge of the net, he swung his body to the right releasing his grip as the net sailed out in a beautiful circle over the water. John's heart beat with excitement as the net descended over the unsuspecting fish. He jerked hard on the cord closing the weights. For a brief moment he experienced nothing. Then the net jerked back and he became aware of the frantic movement of the enclosed fish. He retrieved the net and pulling it out of the water, felt the weight of three large musht, squirming and fighting to free themselves. It was his first solo fishing victory, and he felt like the man they proclaimed him to be at his bar mitzvah.

John scampered out of the water holding the net over his shoulder. When he got to the house, he ran to the back door, shouting for James, his older brother, who had carefully trained John in the art of net casting. James opened the door and smiled at his little brother's triumph.

"I believe you've got it, brother. Now let's see how well you can clean fish. Maybe Momma will cook 'em for lunch."

The well-made cast net was one of John's presents at his recent bar mitzvah, and with his brother's coaching, he had perfected the art of casting on the sandy beach.

James and John were born into a strict Jewish household. Although their father Zebedee was not a Pharisee, he observed all Jewish festivals and strongly believed in keeping the law. He was faithful in living his life according to these legal demands and principles. His home was in Capernaum on the shore of the Sea of Galilee, which defined his occupation. He was the owner of a profitable fishing enterprise, which involved a number of small boats and their hired crews. He sold fresh fish to the towns and villages nearby and well-preserved salted fish to Judea, principally Jerusalem.

Zebedee's occupation was a little too commonplace and commercial for him to be widely accepted in the intellectual circles of Jerusalem, but he was highly respected both for his financial success and his strict Jewish practices. Zebedee had married a much younger woman, Salome of Nazareth. She was a very attractive woman with a sweet and patient disposition, a good match for Zebedee, who possessed a quick temper and a highly dominating personality. She had given him two strong and handsome sons to grow up and share his faith and business. Salome had a bright mind and with the help of Zebedee had become knowledgeable enough to keep the books and records of the fishing business.

Zenedee delivered fish to many prominent people in Jerusalem including the high priest and other members of the Sanhedrin, the highest Jewish deliberative body under Roman rule, commonly called the council. He was thereby well-known by the religious leaders of Israel. It was customary for Zebedee to attend all major Jewish festivals in Jerusalem, where he stayed with his younger brother Malachi, owner of a large home and courtyard.

Malachi, named after the prophet, had studied to be a rabbi. But when the most successful merchant in Jerusalem offered him a job and a share of the business, Malachi couldn't refuse. He had worked hard and his efforts made the business even more profitable.

When the old merchant died with no living relatives, the business passed into Malachi's hands. After his young wife contracted a rare fever and died, Malachi never married again, but put all his energy and time into the enterprise. At fifty, he had accumulated enough wealth to retire.

Both the successful Zebedee businessmen were very intelligent, but were a study in contrast. Unlike his brother, Malachi was open minded, intellectual and an extrovert. His house was always open to Zebedee and Salome, and he doted upon his two nephews, James and John.

Zebedee's sons had the benefit of attending a special Hebrew School for the more prominent and precocious boys of the area. Compared to most Galilean youths, their education was exceptional and even included some Hellenist (Greek) influence. Capernaum was the busiest and largest of the Galilean ports and offered more cultural and religious advantages.

Another post-bar mitzvah experience included the boys' first encounter with their father's fishing fleet. John's first night on the sea was exciting but exhausting. He joined the men letting out the long trammel net and then observed as the boat sailed into the net's loop. The crew beat the boat bottom and splashed oars to scare the fish downward into the net. Then came the long laborious job of pulling the net in and separating the fish. He learned how to clean and repair the nets and at 15 could replace any member of the crew for a night's work. Both John and James became experienced and capable fishermen by their 17th birthdays.

But there were some unusual aspects of John's personality. Although his education and that of his brother was intellectually challenging and their study of Judaism serious, John was developing a keen interest in the more fundamental questions: What was the meaning of life? How could a person really know God? Where was life leading? Although he shared these thoughts with no one, John believed that someday he would find the answers—the *truth*. His good looks and normally friendly disposition belied his serious side, and like his father, he could become antagonistic and rebellious when crossed. With this complex personality, John began his earnest and sustained search for the Infinite.

News of a wild desert man's preaching had traveled all the way to Galilee. Israel had experienced no prophet for over 400 years; consequently much discussion and speculation ensued. The fishermen of Capernaum were no exception. John, always curious and interested, wondered if this event might be a milestone in the long, prophetic history of Judaism. And although his father threw skepticism and even scorn on the subject, John secretly resolved to witness this mysterious figure one day.

The province of Judea was always in a state of political and religious turmoil. Pharisees tended to dominate the religion of Israel, while Saducees worked well with the Romans and advocated compromise and co-existence. The Essenes were monastic and lived by their own rules and strict religious practices; they mostly dwelt off by themselves and bothered no one. The Zealots were constantly at odds with their Roman overlords and secretly advocated rebellion. As long as the Zealots were in a minority, there was no major trouble. The radical nature of the Zealots was a constant source of tension, and most citizens of Judea felt better when the Zealots were well under control.

Many of the prophets of Israel had predicted the coming of a savior, called by some the Anointed One or the Messiah, who would rule Israel in a just and perfect manner. Many believed this event would include overthrowing the Roman occupation and return to Jewish self-rule. Occasionally a person would rise up and make claim to this title only to be crushed by the Romans or lose the following of the people. Most of this tension occurred in Judea and centered itself in Jerusalem.

The province of Galilee was agrarian and somewhat remote from Judea. The main concerns of life there were the farmer's crops or the yield of fish from the Sea of Galilee. However, expectations of a Messiah were also present, and news from Judea made its way into Galilee and was widely discussed especially among the younger people. That is why the fishermen of Zebedee talked at length about the unusual desert preacher. The topic kept John anxious to experience the preacher's message.

5

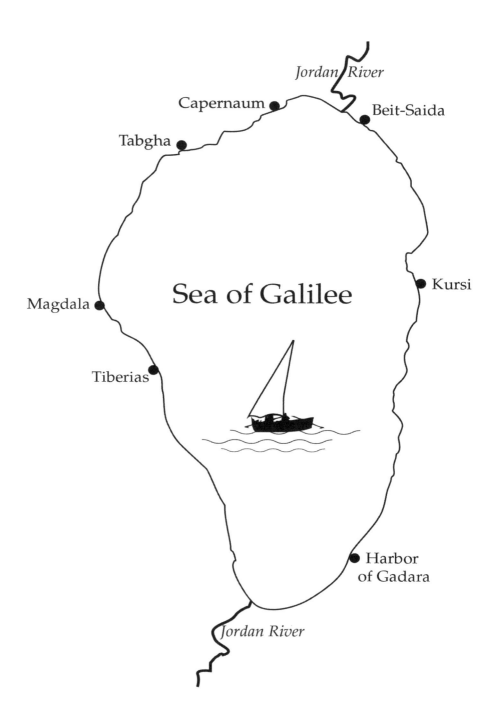

Jordan River

Capernaum

Beit-Saida

Tabgha

Kursi

Magdala

Sea of Galilee

Tiberias

Harbor
of Gadara

Jordan River

II

The Crucial Journey

By the time James and John reached eighteen, they were entrusted by Zebedee to deliver fish, both to the surrounding villages and to Jerusalem. In order to prepare fish for the more distant cities, they were preserved by salting. The port of Magdala, only seven miles southwest of Capernaum, became the center for salting fish. When the supply of salted fish grew low, Zebedee's boats would dock at Magdala and unload. After being salted, the fish were then picked up at Magdala before the longer trip to Judea could begin. John and James took turns at this task.

Samaria, the province between Galilee and Judea, lay on the west side of the Jordan River. About 722 BC the province was overrun by Assyria with many Samaritans carried off to foreign lands. Colonists from Assyria were brought in and intermarried with the native Samaritans. Some aspects of pagan religion were also introduced, and Samaria became a country of mixed races and religion. Much later the people turned more to Judaism, but designated Mount Gerizim as the center of worship instead of Jerusalem. Jews would not associate with Samaritans for they considered them to be a mixed race with different religious practices. For this reason Galilean Jews traveling to Judea forded the Jordan River north of the sea and took the eastern road to the south.

When John's turn came, he harnessed the two burros and set out early in the morning for Magdala. Spring had come, bringing out wild flowers and all the freshness of the land. John drank in the beauty of the red ball of sun rising over the eastern sea until its rays danced upon the water. It was a pleasant trip and if he kept a fast pace, he could make it back to Capernaum late the same day.

Magdala, being a small harbor town, John's arrival touched off many friendly greetings from his friends and associates. After loading the burros with salted fish, neatly packaged in ten pound sacks, he was back on the road to Capernaum. His only pause was to enjoy the lunch prepared for him by his mother Salome. He tied the burros out on a fresh patch of grass and enjoyed the brief respite before returning to Capernaum.

Before sun-up the following day John was well on his way to the northern tip of the sea. He carefully guided the burros over the ford of the Jordan River, and turned south on the road to Judea. Again the trip beside the sea was pleasant, and he passed through several small harbor towns. As evening approached, he entered the harbor of Gadara, where he spent the night at the house of Zebedee's relatives.

Rising early the next morning, John left the sea and took the road paralleling the Jordan River, which he followed for the next three days, camping out at night under a beautiful canopy of stars. He particularly enjoyed this part of the trip as he loved all aspects of nature and awakened to a soft spring breeze. His eyes caught the motion of a majestic golden eagle plunging to the river bank to snare its prey, and he mused, "If only I could capture the answers to my questions as easily."

He had brought two loaves of bread, and he feasted on them and the salt-fish. Bathing in the river invigorated him, and he was ready to set out again.

Toward the middle of the fourth day John caught up with some other travelers. He soon struck up a conversation. "Where are you fellows headed?"

"Haven't you heard?" they answered. "The Prophet has begun preaching again. We're going there to be baptized."

John's interest immediately picked up. "You've heard the wild man?"

"His dress might be wild, but his speech is anything but. He is calling all who will listen to repentance, back to the Living God, to a life of purity and dedication."

"Where does this take place?" John asked.

"Another five miles down the river at Bethany. He usually shows up early in the morning. Coming out of the Judean Wilderness, he wades to a rock in the river and begins to preach."

John's curiosity was now completely aroused. "We've heard much about him. Do you mind if I join up with you?" Sensing that the friendly, good natured young man with the loaded burros was no danger to them, the pilgrims agreed with his request to join them.

At Bethany, after a somewhat fitful sleep, John could hardly wait for morning to break. At daylight he hurriedly joined the crowd which was beginning to form. There were wealthy Jews from Jerusalem in their fine garments and the poor from Galilee and the countryside. There were young and old and people of many different occupations. John wondered, "Would the desert preacher have any real answers for my search?"

Suddenly an audible gasp went up from the crowd gathered on both banks of the Jordan. Excitedly, John gazed across the river.

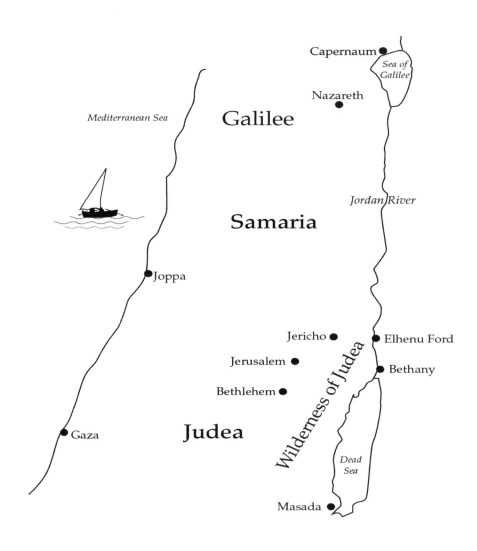

III

The Prophet

He came striding out of the Wilderness of Judea. His large frame was gaunt but powerfully built. His beard was long, his hair longer and gathered into a pony tail reaching to his waist. He wore a large animal hide held up at one shoulder and drawn in at the waist by a leather strap. In his right hand he carried a stout staff, and on his feet he wore sandals of animal skin secured by leather thongs.

He waded into the water and climbed a rock close to the middle of the river. He then began to preach. His voice was deep and robust, and his words resonated with prophetic and apocalyptic phrases.

"I come to proclaim a baptism of repentance for the forgiveness of sins, as it is written by the Prophet Isaiah:

'The voice of one crying out in the wilderness:

"Prepare the way of the Lord,
make his paths straight.
Every valley shall be filled,
and every mountain and hill shall be made low,
and the crooked shall be made straight,
and the rough ways made smooth;
and all flesh shall see the salvation of God."'

"You brood of vipers! Who warned you to flee from the wrath to come? Bear fruits worthy of repentance. Do not presume to say to yourselves, 'We have Abraham as our ancestor'; for I tell you, God is able from these stones to raise up children to Abraham. Even now the ax is lying at the root of the trees; every tree therefore that does not bear good fruit is cut down and thrown into the fire."

Just then someone in the crowd shouted, "What then must we do?"

John (the Baptist) replied, "Whoever has two coats must share with one who has none; and whoever has food must do the same."

A tax collector, who came to be baptized, asked, "Rabbi, what should I do?"

"Collect only what is prescribed for you."

Finally, a soldier asked, "And what are we soldiers to do?"

"Do not extort money by threats or false accusations. Be satisfied with what you are paid."

After the questions, the Baptist raised his arms in an expression of praise to God. Then in his robust voice he shouted, "Come!"

After a brief pause, one man slowly waded forward to the Prophet, who had left his staff on the rock and descended into the water. The Baptist gently placed one hand on his head and the other over his mouth and nose and pushed him backward under the water of the Jordan. As he baptized him he spoke an inaudible prayer. Then another came and soon a line had formed.

John watched as more than a hundred were baptized. He then untied his burros and headed for Jerusalem. He had fish to deliver to the high priest and other dignitaries. But his head kept spinning as he recalled the words and actions of the Prophet.

IV

Destination Jerusalem

In order to ford the Jordan in springtime, John had to travel back five miles to the north. He forded the River at el-Henu, taking the road to Jericho, where he spent the night. From that town to Jerusalem, the road was a well traveled mountain route. When John reached the summit of the Mount of Olives ridge, the panoramic view of the Ancient City spread out before him. He loved this view with the age old surrounding walls and towers and the glistening temple towering above all. The sight always lifted John's spirit as if it welcomed him to the city.

He passed through the Water Gate and headed for the Upper City where the high priest's palace was located. The guard on the gate was well known to John and waved him through to the servant's entrance. He was greeted warmly by the kitchen help, who were expecting a visit from the young fisherman.

"How many sacks this time?" John asked the cook, a middle aged Jewish matron.

"The same three should last until James makes his visit."

"Where is Deborah?" John sheepishly inquired.

"I knew you'd want to see her," the cook replied. "She's working in the other end of the house. I'll go get her."

John had met Deborah, one of the house maids of the Palace, on a previous visit. She had a slim but full figure with long black hair falling to her shoulders. Her face was well proportioned with beautiful features, and her eyes were large and dark. A few years younger than John, the two felt an immediate attraction for each other. They talked only briefly in the kitchen, and she had walked out to see him off. John, however, had thought of her many times since that first meeting.

When she entered the room, her beauty again amazed John. They exchanged formal but friendly greetings and Miriam, the palace cook, asked them to sit at a table in the kitchen. It was about lunch time so she prepared plates for the couple. Over lunch John related the events of his trip and asked, "Have you heard about the desert preacher?"

"I've heard that a mysterious man who comes from the wilderness is preaching again at the Jordan," Deborah replied, "but that's all I know."

John then related the events which led him to the Baptist's gathering.

"I've never heard anyone like him. He is sure to cause a stir among the religious community here in Jerusalem."

"What does he preach about?"

"He castigates the present attitudes and climate of our religion and calls for repentance and a new unselfish life of Godly dedication—perhaps in preparation for some coming momentous event."

The conversation drifted to Deborah and her family. She

was the daughter of a poor but respected family in Jerusalem. Her father had died the year before, and she had been fortunate to get a job in the high priest's palace. One advantage of this employment was the education she was picking up while working in and around the classes for Hebrew boys. Besides her mother, she had a brother and a sister who were older and also worked to support the family.

The time passed quickly and it was soon time for John to leave and begin his afternoon deliveries. They clasped hands firmly and looked deeply into each other's eyes as John bade his goodbye. Miriam paid John for the fish and told him not to be too long in returning.

His other deliveries mostly to members of the Sanhedrin went routinely, and by nightfall he entered his uncle's house, where he was warmly greeted and got a good night's rest. Before sunrise the next morning he was on his way back to Capernaum. When he came to the Jordan, he forded it, turned north, and headed for home along the river. But he resolved to come back and hear the Baptist again as soon as his duties permitted.

V

Baptism

It was early evening on the day John returned to Capernaum. Salome had supper prepared and when they were seated, after Zebedee's blessing she immediately asked John about his trip to Jerusalem. He was reticent to talk about Deborah, but very eager to tell about the Prophet. James and Salome listened attentively as John described the Prophet, recounted his words, and told about the large number of pilgrims baptized. But Zebedee was restless throughout the discussion and effectively closed it by pronouncing that the Baptist was most likely an opportunist seeking publicity and support of the people—possibly another Messiah pretender. John was taken aback and shocked by his father's harsh contentions, but he knew better than to argue with the old orthodox Jew.

After supper John literally ran all the way to Simon Peter's house. Even though he was four years older, Simon was his best friend and with his younger brother, Andrew, commanded one of the boats in Zebedee's fleet. Entering the house he embraced the big fisherman, who said, "Where've you been, John? We missed you the last few days." The two close friends sat down and John related the story of the Baptist.

"Simon, you've got to hear him. I believe he is a prophet or maybe even more."

"Well, that's going to be hard for me to do. I've also got some news for you. I've asked Rachel to marry me, and her father has agreed to our betrothal."

John immediately recalled the pretty, young girl. "Well, congratulations friend! I never thought you'd be tied down. But she is a beauty. When is this to take place?"

"The date hasn't been set yet, but neither of us want a long engagement."

"I'm not tied down, and I'm very interested," shouted Andrew from the adjoining room where he had overheard the conversation. "Maybe we can get off sometimes next month and go to hear this mysterious preacher."

John was both elated at Simon Peter's surprising announcement and disappointed that his best friend's new status would not permit him to make the trip.

Two weeks went by with John returning to his father's boat. Then one of the last cold fronts of spring came through with strong winds and bad weather. The boats would not put out for four to five days or longer. John contacted Andrew and they planned to leave early the next morning. Being young and strong and carrying a minimum of supplies, they made fast time, traveling into the night before retiring for a few hours of sleep. By the end of the third day, they were close to Bethany where the Prophet was baptizing. Early the next morning they joined the crowd and were awaiting the arrival of the Baptist.

This time his strong voice could be heard just before he appeared on the river bank:

> "*Prepare the way of the Lord*
> *Make his paths straight*
> *Every valley shall be filled,*
> *And every mountain and hill shall be made low,*
> *And the crooked shall be made straight*
> *And the rough ways made smooth;*
> *And all flesh shall see the salvation of God*"

Then he burst forth upon the scene seemingly bigger than life itself. He wore the same animal skins, had the same long hair and beard, and carried the same stout staff. Climbing the rock, he recited many verses of scripture from the prophets. They all spoke of the Day of Judgment and were filled with apocalyptic warnings. He continued:

> "*We all like sheep have gone astray;*
> *we have all turned to our own way....*"

But then he spoke words John had not heard before:

> "*I baptize you with water for repentance, but one who is more powerful than I is coming after me; I am not worthy to carry his sandals. He will baptize you with the Holy Spirit and fire. His winnowing fork is in his hand, and he will clear his threshing floor and will gather his*

wheat into the granary; but the chaff he will burn with unquenchable fire."

And after that, in his large robust voice: "COME AND REPENT WHILE YOU CAN, FOR THE KINGDOM OF GOD IS AT HAND!"

He then held his arms and staff high and began a prayer which could not be heard. John whispered to Andrew, "I'm going down."

"I'm right behind you," his friend replied.

VI

Fateful Decision

After their baptism and taking their place in the crowd again, Andrew said to John, "Do you feel any different?"

John thought for a moment and then replied, "I do feel cleaner inside, more alive, and more inclined to make a commitment."

"You couldn't have put my feelings in better words."

Even though Simon Peter was his best friend, John had always considered Andrew to be conscientious and serious concerning his dedication to Judaism. The young man was two years older than John and two years younger than Simon. His build was tall and slender, and he wore his hair in a short pigtail. Although overshadowed by Simon, he was an able fisherman and was known to possess a mind of his own.

In order to journey back home without missing any work, the two youths took off immediately for Capernaum. They again made fast time returning and arrived home late on the third day. Fortunately for them, it turned out that the weather had kept the boats at anchor for six days, and they reported for work that same night.

John worked hard as usual, doing even more than his share, but his heart was not in it. He kept thinking about the last part of the Baptist's address. Just who was the preacher talking about—the one who would baptize with the Holy Spirit and fire? Could it be that the Baptist had some spiritual intuition or knowledge about the coming Messiah? The young fisherman just had to find out, for there was no doubt in his mind that the Baptist was really a prophet. Although he loved the sea, his family, and the beautiful land of Galilee, a deeper feeling stirred within him. Somehow, he felt he had to return to the Prophet. He could not miss the coming of the Anointed One. He believed that all his life had pointed him in this direction. His search for *truth* must take precedence over all other considerations.

Consequently, he determined to talk to his father that night. He knew it would be difficult since his father had continued to disparage and speak contemptuously about the "wild, desert preacher."

After supper that night, he asked for a private conversation with Zebedee. John began, "Father, I owe you everything. You've seen to my good education, my advancement in the faith, given me a loving home and trained me in a useful and honorable occupation. That is why it is so difficult for me to tell you..."

The old man's eyes narrowed and he gazed apprehensively upon his son.

"Father, I must leave you and Mother, James, and the business. I feel strongly that I've been called to seek out the *truth* and my own commitment to it."

Zebedee interrupted, "Has this anything to do with the so-called desert prophet?" John could feel the heavy scorn in his father's voice.

"Yes, I believe he has the clue to my search, and I must seek him out and attempt somehow to fulfill my deepest yearning."

"You would leave your family who loves you, your friends, and your business for *this*? Isn't the faith of our fathers, the faith Adonai has given us sufficient?"

"Father, you know how long it's been since we've experienced a real prophet? Judaism has nourished me, but as the ancient prophets have predicted, God is going to do something new, something we cannot even imagine. I believe *that* time is drawing near. The Baptist has convinced me of it."

Zebedee looked disconsolate, deflated. He sensed the enthusiasm and determination in his son's words.

"If this is what you must do, get on with it. But I believe you are making a grave mistake. I hate to see you disillusioned, and have to come crawling back and admit you were chasing ghosts or worse."

"I'm leaving in the morning, so I'll tell you goodbye now. Never doubt my love and appreciation for you." John stood up, crossed over to his father and hugged him, but the old man said nothing, showed little emotion, and appeared whipped and tired.

Salome reacted a little differently. He found her still in the kitchen with James, cleaning the utensils. John repeated his desires and decision. Salome's tone was more tender and pleading, and she had tears in her eyes. She understood her son's feelings, but she didn't want to contradict her husband, for she knew what his attitude was. James was understanding and sympathetic and even perhaps a little envious.

Afterward, John expressed his love, embraced his mother and his brother warmly and promised they would hear from him.

"Goodbye, little brother," James said, "and the Lord go with you."

John then went to Simon Peter and Andrew's house. He sat down with his two friends and repeated his decision. Simon, who had not experienced the Prophet, said sadly, "I just hope you and Andrew know what you are doing." Surprised, John turned to Andrew.

"That's right, John. I've talked it over with Simon. I plan to leave also. We can begin together in the morning." It was a much easier decision for Andrew. The two brother's parents had passed away several years earlier, and Andrew had no business to inherit. Peter was also much more understanding than Zebedee. He embraced the two youths warmly and told them to take care and keep in touch.

VII

The Disciples

Very early the next morning, John accompanied by his friend Andrew, began his third trip to Bethany. After an uneventful journey, they again joined the crowds at the Jordan. The Baptist arrived at the appointed hour and recited many verses from the prophets of Israel before announcing the coming move of God. After the baptisms and after most of the people had left, John and Andrew decided to follow the Prophet, who made his way back into the Judean Wilderness. They entered the barren wasteland of sand and rocks, but stayed well behind and moved as quietly as possible.

Suddenly he stepped from behind a rock, confronting them; he held his staff in a defensive position.

"Why do you follow me?"

Collecting his senses, John replied, "Sir, we came to seek you out, to become followers if you would permit it."

"Who are you? And where do you come from?"

Again John answered, "We are fishermen from Capernaum. I am John Bar Zebedee (son of Zebedee) and this is my friend, Andrew. We were both baptized a little more than a week ago."

"Yes, I recall it now. But you have never lived as I do."

"We're both young and strong and willing to learn."

The Baptist paused for a few moments. The young men seemed to be sincere, and perhaps he could use some help with the ever growing number of candidates for baptism.

"Well, come along and we'll discuss it further."

They were already approaching a higher elevation with bare and desolate rolling hills. Ahead John caught sight of a dark opening in the hill side. Was this the home of the Prophet? He had guessed right. It was a large cave; a charcoal fire still smoldered just inside.

"I know you boys are as hungry as I am. I have no meat, but you are welcomed to what I have."

Hanging from a line secured at each end to the wall was a collection of roots. And underneath was a gourd filled with dried dates from the Judean palms. In the back of the cave, clear water dripped from the rocks into a larger gourd. Carefully watching the Prophet, the boys followed behind, picking some of the same "food" that he had chosen. Another large gourd was filled with honey. Their host dipped some of the roots into the gourd and they did likewise.

Although strange, the "food" tasted amazingly good and they had soon eaten their fill.

"Now," spoke the Baptist, "let's hear some more about you two. What are you seeking?"

Andrew, who until then had been silent, spoke first. "Sir, we heard you speak of some great coming event of God, and we believe you to be a prophet. We are here because we seek to learn from you."

"We have grown up in the faith; orthodox Judaism has been poured into me since before I could read," added John. "Yet somehow I feel there is a more human—a less legalistic aspect we have missed."

"If there is more, and you seem to speak of God's imminent move, we don't want to miss it," Andrew asserted.

"That's it, Sir. We want to learn from you. We are willing to help you in any way we can," John put in enthusiastically.

The Baptist stood and walked to the cave mouth. He stared up into the starry sky for several long moments. He then walked back and put more wood on the fire.

Finally he spoke, "Your families, your work—won't you be missed?"

"I have talked with my mother, my father and brother, and though they don't really understand, they have acquiesced. My father will simply hire another hand to take my place," John explained.

"My father and mother are dead," Andrew offered, "and my brother can find a replacement for me on the boat. He too doesn't fully understand, for he hasn't heard you preach, and right now he's hopelessly obsessed with his soon-to-be bride."

"Well, you appear to be honest and sincere. I've lived alone in this desert for years, so maybe it's time I had some help. We'll give it a try if you can take my kind of life."

The boys were greatly relieved and pleased at the Prophet's decision. They were thrilled at the prospect of living and learning from a real prophet of Israel, and their expectations ran high. They slept well that night on their mats of camel hair. Their dreams were filled with visions of experiencing unusual and miraculous events.

VIII

The Life Of A Prophet

The next morning, after a hearty breakfast of the same food, the three were making the short trek back to the river. Crowds had already formed and were awaiting the Baptist. After his dire quotations from the prophets and his pronouncement of the Coming One, the Prophet began baptizing. Late winter and spring rains had swelled the river making the current swifter. John stood on one side of the Jordan and Andrew on the other. They helped the elderly and infirmed into the water and escorted them to the Prophet. The baptisms lasted into the early afternoon until the crowd at last dispersed.

Finally only the three were left standing on the west bank. The Prophet disappeared into the desert, telling the boys to meet him back at the cave. When he returned early in the evening, he brought a skin filled with freshly dressed meat.

31

"I know your diets include meat, so I went hunting. My vows restrict me from eating meat."

After the exertions of the day the boys were indeed hungry. They strung the meat on sticks and held it over the fire. They were reluctant to ask their host what sort of animal it had come from, and even the thought was a little unsettling. However, their confidence in the Baptist quickly overcame their apprehension, and roasted over the charcoal the meat was delicious. The Baptist ate his roots and honey.

After supper, as they sat around the fire, the Baptist began quoting from memory excerpts from Jeremiah, Isaiah, and Amos. He would stop every once in a while and ask a question. A lively discussion would ensue with the two young men trying to show the Prophet their knowledge of scripture. Sometimes the discussion would turn argumentative. John hotly defended his position indicating his inherent volatility. The holy man would let the words of the youths play out. Then he would sum up the subject with his remarkable interpretation. His memory was incredible, showing years of familiarity and analysis of the texts. The session was ended in prayer with each one contributing.

One night after a particularly rousing debate, John could not sleep, and he arose and sat close to the fire thinking through the heated discussion. Feeling a hand upon his shoulder, he turned to see the Baptist smiling down at him. "John you have the tenacity and eye of an eagle. Some day you will use this talent for the glory of God." Such a statement coming from a prophet of God quieted John's feelings, and he retired to a sound night's sleep.

The Baptist gave special emphasis to the prophets, not only the severe warnings, but passages which emphasized mercy, love, sincerity, and justice. This was in contrast to the tedious, hard to follow, perfunctory rules of the Pharisees. He stressed righteousness—such as in Amos:

> *I despise your festivals,*
> *And I take no delight in your solemn assemblies.*
> *Even though you offer me your burnt offerings and grain offerings, I will not accept them....*
> *But let justice roll down like waters,*
> *and righteousness like an ever flowing stream.*

Isaiah was perhaps his most quoted— as in:

> *Look, you serve your own interest on your fast day....*
> *Look, you fast only to quarrel and to fight*
> *And to strike with a wicked fist;*
> *Such fasting as you do today will not make your voice heard on high....*
> *Is not this the fast that I choose:*
> *to loose the bonds of injustice,*
> *to undo the thongs of the yoke,*
> *to let the oppressed go free,*
> *and to break every yoke?*
> *Is it not to share your bread with the hungry,*
> *and bring the homeless poor into your house;*
> *When you see the naked, to cover them,*
> *and not to hide yourself from your own kin?*
> *Then your light shall break forth like the dawn...*
> *Then you shall call, and the Lord will answer....*

The young men were always anxious to learn about the coming of the Anointed One, with their questions of who and when. But the Baptist would always gently steer them away from the subject. They were not yet ready to approach that question.

This same routine continued throughout the summer, the mornings being filled with the profound words of the Prophet addressed to the pilgrims, followed by baptisms. The boys' afternoons were spent swimming and fishing in the Jordan or exploring the unusual landscape of the desert, which ranged from mountains or towering hills to wave after wave of desert sand. They even discovered a wadi that dropped 300 feet to a small stream bed winding its way to the river.

The Baptist preferred his solitude after an exhausting number of baptisms. He would go off alone to pray and meditate, listening for the Spirit to speak. Occasionally, he would hunt in a way never revealed to the youths, but would usually return with fresh meat to roast. At other times, he and the boys would dig roots, rob wild honey, or visit a grove of Judean date palms to replenish their supply. Sometimes they placed dates in the sun to dry, providing for the winter and spring.

Gradually, some of the Baptist's past would unfold. He was the son of a Jewish priest, Zechariah and his wife Elizabeth. Although, they had prayed for a son for years, Elizabeth was barren. John was born to them after both had passed the normal age of child bearing and were approaching old age. Extraordinary events accompanied his birth. Angels and prophesies were involved in naming him John and predicting his future holy calling. He was said to be filled with the Holy Spirit at birth.

Since his parents were elderly at his infancy, they had died by the time John reached twelve. He was "adopted" by the Essenes at Qumran in the desert. Consequently, he had been reared in a celibate, austere, and monastic life style dedicated to God and experiencing ritual washings.

By the time he turned twenty, the Spirit called him away

from Qumran to live a solitary, God-focused life. It was gradually revealed to him that he was to announce the coming of the Messiah and to prepare his way. He did not know who the Messiah was, but he received the message that when the time came, he would be given an unmistakable sign.

Actually none of this surprised the two boys. It was totally in keeping with what they had expected. The Baptist also gradually made it clear that the time for this miraculous move of God was drawing near.

IX

The Time Draws Near

By early fall the young men were also quoting passages from the prophets. Gradually their complete confidence in the Baptist's teaching had grown as had their devotion and respect. They now usually addressed him as "Master." There were even times John entertained the idea that the Baptist might turn out to be the Messiah.

Their evening lessons turned more to passages directly related to the Coming One and the expectation and excitement of the young disciples increased. The Baptist was aglow with the fire of faith as he recited Isaiah:

> *"...in the latter time he will make glorious, the way of the sea, the land beyond the Jordan, Galilee of the nations. The people who walked in darkness have seen a great light, those who lived in a land of deep darkness—on them the light has*

shined...For a child has been born for us; a son given to us; authority rests upon his shoulders, and he is named Wonderful Counselor, Mighty God, everlasting Father, Prince of Peace."

And on another night:

"A shoot shall come out from the stump of Jesse (father of David) and a branch shall grow out of his roots. The spirit of the Lord shall rest on him, the spirit of wisdom and understanding, the spirit of counsel and might, the spirit of knowledge and the fear of the Lord. His delight shall be in the fear of the Lord. He shall not judge by what his eyes see, or decide by what his ears hear; but with righteousness he shall judge the poor and decide with equity for the meek of the earth. He shall strike the earth with the rod of his mouth."

But perhaps his favorite and most repeated quotation:

"Behold my Servant Whom I uphold, my elect in Whom My soul delights! I have put my Spirit upon Him; He will bring fourth justice and right and reveal truth to the nations....
"It is too light a thing that you should be my Servant to raise up the tribes of Jacob and to restore the survivors of Israel. I will also give You for a light to the nations, that My salvation may extend to the end of the earth."

The Baptist then spoke more freely for the first time about the coming Messiah. He told the young disciples that he did not know the identity of the Servant of God. He explained that the Spirit had made it known that an unmistakable sign would point Him out. He made it clear to them that even though he had been their master, that the Coming One would be greater—that He must increase and that the Prophet must decrease.

"This is why I have not spoken to you about it. I simply did not know the answer to who and when. I still don't, but the Spirit indicates to me that the time is drawing closer."

X

The Revealing

Each day after the previous night's discussion, John and Andrew caught themselves carefully looking over the pilgrims. Somewhere perhaps among them was the *One* Israel had expected for several hundred years. Would he come to be baptized by the Prophet? Or would he be revealed at a later time? A week went by with nothing unusual happening.

On the first day of the following week, John noticed a group of richly dressed men. Some of them wore the distinguishing garments of the Pharisees. John wondered what they were doing in the wilderness. They kept to the rear of the crowd and when the last pilgrim was baptized, they approached the Prophet.

A balding middle aged man stepped forward and spoke, "We are a delegation from the council in Jerusalem. We were sent here to inquire about who you are and why you are baptizing such large numbers of Jews."

The Baptist sensed the tension and even the belligerence in the Pharisee's voice. He declined to answer immediately.

"Who are you?" the man repeated. "Are you the Messiah?"

The Baptist answered, "I am not."

"Well, are you Elijah?" (The Jews believed Elijah would return before the Messiah.)

He answered, "No, I am not."

"Then, who are you? We need to have an answer for those who sent us."

John the Baptist answered, "I am the voice of one crying in the wilderness. Make straight the way of the Lord, just as the prophet Isaiah said."

"Then why are you baptizing?"

John answered them, "I baptize with water for repentance. Among you stands a stranger, one you do not know. He is coming after me, and I am not worthy to carry his sandals. He will baptize with the Holy Spirit and fire."

John turned and walked away into the desert. John Bar Zebedee and Andrew followed.

The group of scribes and Pharisees were left mumbling to each other.

The next day a young Jew stood in line waiting to approach the Baptist. His complexion was tanned from the sun, and his well trimmed beard was brown. His features were generally handsome; his dark brown eyes seemed to convey a sense of friendliness and understanding. Even so, he did not stand out in the crowd. Yet there was something in his bearing—not haughty but commanding, which might have suggested a rabbi. Under a simple garment he possessed muscular shoulders, and his arms and hands showed signs of manual labor. He had not drawn any special attention.

He was a cousin of the Prophet, although neither had seen

the other since early childhood. The Prophet baptized him as he would any other, but when he came up out of the water, in a blinding flash of light the Baptist distinctly saw something resembling a dove descend upon the young Jew and remain on him.

Numbers of people standing by including John Bar Zebedee witnessed the light and the strange dove-like phenomenon. A hush came over the crowd as they stared in awe at the stranger. Just then a voice like thunder was heard pronouncing, "This is my Son, the Beloved with whom I am well pleased."

The Baptist lifted his arms in praise. The descending dove lighting upon the stranger was the sign previously revealed to the Prophet. "You should have baptized me," he stated reverently.

Jesus replied, "Let it be so for now. For it is proper to fulfill all righteousness."

John's heart was beating with so much excitement he could hardly contain it. Andrew also had seen and heard it all, and his elation was overpowering. The crowd was still hushed and every eye was on the young Jew who, to the amazement of all, waded out of the water and strode off into the Judean desert.

That evening the young men had many questions to ask the Baptist. But the most he could say was that his part in the preparation and revealing of the Messiah was accomplished. However, he would continue his baptisms until the Spirit gave him further guidance.

The next few days were anticlimactic, but the crowds kept coming and the baptisms were continued. No one reported having seen the stranger, and the excitement of the unusual events gradually died down.

Finally six weeks later, Jesus walked out of the wilderness and joined the crowd. His appearance was gaunt and somewhat disheveled. He looked as if he had been in the desert for days without sufficient nourishment. As he walked by, the Baptist exclaimed, "Behold the Lamb of God who takes away the sin of the world! He on whom we saw the Spirit descend and remain is the one who baptizes with the Holy Spirit. And I myself tell you that this is the Son of God."

The next day Jesus, now washed and groomed, walked again by the Baptist who was talking with John and Andrew. The Prophet again exclaimed. "Look, here is the Lamb of God."

The two young disciples started to follow Jesus, but looked back at their Master. He smiled and nodded at them as if to say, "It's alright. He's your new Master. You must follow Him."

PART II

John And Jesus

XI

The Calling

When Jesus saw the two disciples of John following him he turned and asked, "What are you looking for?"

John Bar Zebedee answered, "Rabbi, where are you staying?"

"Come with me and see." Jesus replied.

The two boys stayed with him the rest of the day and spent the night. They had many questions, and Jesus began to open the scriptures to them. Following the excellent preparation by the Baptist, Jesus made many more things clear to them.

The next morning Jesus decided to journey to Galilee. The two young disciples were glad to be headed home to Capernaum after spending the spring and summer at Bethany. But Jesus knew exactly what he was doing; he knew that Galilee was the place he would find more disciples. The people of Galilee were "of the land and sea," unspoiled by the temptations of city life and generally unaffected by the extreme legalism of the Pharisees.

Upon arriving in Capernaum, Jesus told the young men to visit their homes and families. Andrew immediately found Simon, who had married Rachel during the summer. Andrew greeted her with a hug and expressed warm congratulations and best wishes to his new sister. After she had excused herself, he related the events of the summer, and exclaimed, "Brother, we have found the Anointed One. You must come immediately and meet him."

Simon long ago had learned to respect his younger brother's judgment, so he followed Andrew to where they had left Jesus, who said to him, "I understand you are Simon, the son of Jona. From now on you will be called Peter."

John had likewise found James and brought him to the Teacher. The five of them were engaged in lively conversation when Philip's name was mentioned. As soon as Jesus heard about Philip, he asked, "Can one of you bring Philip to me?" Andrew volunteered since Philip lived close to Peter's house.

When Philip heard the good news, he went to find his friend, Nathanael, and exclaimed, "John and Andrew have found the Messiah, the one Moses and the prophets wrote about, Jesus of Nazareth."

"Can anything good come out of Nazareth?" Nathanael asked.

Philip replied, "Let us go and see."

After they joined the others, Jesus addressed Nathanael, "You are indeed an Israelite in whom there is no deceit. I saw you sitting and meditating under the fig tree before Philip called you."

Stunned, Nathanael replied, "Rabbi, you are the Son of God, the King of Israel."

To which Jesus answered, "You will experience much

greater things than this when you follow the Son of Man."

And so the next four disciples were contacted by Jesus, all from the town of Capernaum. All were honest and sincere men of the beautiful, agrarian province of Galilee.

That afternoon all of the disciples returned home to their own families. Jesus also returned to Nazareth, where he greeted his mother Mary and his brothers. Joseph, Mary's husband, had passed away two years earlier.

Peter and Andrew arrived at their home and Peter asked Rachel to join them. Andrew again related the events of the last summer, and then with even greater excitement announced that he and John had found the Messiah. Rachel also was excited, but she wondered what this discovery would mean for Peter. Later that night after they had retired, Peter confessed to Rachel that he might have to be away for some extended periods of time. Rachel was afraid that this might be coming, and she trembled with anxiety at the thought of her new husband's absence. But, as a loyal and supportive wife as well as a faithful woman, she only said a quiet prayer, "Good Lord, please protect him."

John and James also headed for home, but it was unclear in John's mind if he would be welcomed. He recalled with some bitterness the attitude of his father, Zebedee. Salome welcomed him with open arms and tears in her eyes.

"Where is father?" John inquired.

"He's in the bedroom half asleep," she replied.

"Has he forgiven me for leaving?"

"I'm afraid not. If anything he's grown more bitter and withdrawn."

Fearing the worst, John entered the bedroom.

"Your son has returned to greet you, father."

"I have but one son—James," the old man weakly replied.

"But father, I have so much to tell you, so much to explain." The old Jew closed his eyes and turned away.

John realized that any further communication was impossible, at least for the time being. He sadly and somewhat angrily left the room.

John sought out James and asked him to go for a walk in the night air.

Starting with his encounter with the Baptist, he related the summer's experiences. He accorded the Prophet his greatest respect and admiration and explained the unusual life led by the three of them. He told about the hundreds of pilgrims who had been baptized and about his eager expectation of the coming Messiah. He described in vivid detail the baptism of Jesus and the miraculous events accompanying it.

"Jesus is gathering disciples, James, and I pray you will follow him."

"I have given much thought to such a life, brother. In fact, I was jealous of your leaving to seek the truth about the Messiah. I guess we're much alike, and I will pray about it tonight."

When they returned home, Zebedee had retired, and the brothers spent much time talking with Salome. John excitedly told her about Jesus, about His being pointed out as the Messiah. He indicated what a momentous time this was for the Jewish nation and that he was so fortunate to have been accepted by the Master. James also shared in the enthusiasm about the Anointed One. Salome realized that she might lose her other son as well. The thought was a bitter-sweet one, but she was ambitious for both of them and shared in the hope and aspirations concerning the Messiah.

Finally, James jumped up and said, "I've almost forgotten! I'm keeping my crew waiting; we've got to go fishing. Want to come along, little brother?" The thought of spending a night on the water indulging in physical exertion was attractive to John. After changing clothes, he and James rushed off to the boats. Peter and Andrew had gotten the same idea. For John and Andrew, fishing was in their blood, and it would provide a refreshing respite from the routine they had been following.

Greeting their ex-shipmates and working the nets was an exhilarating experience for the two former fishermen. Their luck was also good, and both boats brought in a good haul of fish. In the early morning the fishermen were sitting on the beach mending their nets. With rapt attention on their work, they had not noticed a figure walking toward them until John looked up and exclaimed, "It is the Master. He's coming this way."

When Jesus drew near, he called out, "Peter and Andrew, John and James, come follow me. I will make you fishers of men."

Without hesitation, the four fishermen dropped their nets and followed Jesus.

XII

Signs Of The Messiah

There was a wedding in Cana, a town, in the vicinity of Nazareth, only a few short miles from Capernaum. The marriage celebration was a great occasion for Jews of the first century. It was a time of great rejoicing for family and friends, and sometimes the celebration lasted several days. Mary and Jesus' brothers were invited, as were Jesus and his six disciples, who had been meeting regularly, listening to the Master's teaching.

Jesus, greatly enjoying the festivities and seeing many friends he had grown up with, was suddenly summoned by Mary. John, who often stayed close to the Master, noticed and followed them to a hall outside. Mary, greatly disturbed, told Jesus that the wine had run out. This would have been a shameful oversight on the part of the host and a great embarrassment as well. Jesus, however, answered in a strange way.

"What has that got to do with me, woman. My time has not yet come." Mary, seemingly undistracted, called the servants and instructed them to obey Jesus.

In the hall were six large stone water jars, each holding about thirty gallons. They commonly were used for Jewish purification rites. Jesus told the servants, "Fill the jars with water to the brim, then draw out a cup and take it to the chief steward." John was as puzzled as the servants, but they followed Jesus' instruction. When the steward tasted the water now turned to wine, he was surprised and exclaimed, "The host usually serves the best wine first and saves the inferior for when the guests have drunk their fill. But you have saved the best until now." This amazing miracle was the first sign Jesus performed at the beginning of his ministry. John was a witness and began to understand the amazing power of his Master.

After the wedding celebration, Jesus, accompanied by his disciples, began preaching in the synagogues of Galilee. He interpreted the scriptures, preached the good news of the kingdom of God, and healed every kind of disease. During a year of this remarkable ministry, his fame spread throughout the region and even into Syria, and many people believed in him. When he discerned honesty, sincerity, and depth of character in an individual, he would call him to be a disciple. He even called Matthew, a tax collector, because Jesus could tell what was in the heart of men. The disciples at first were dismayed by his calling, but in time came to recognize Matthew's true heart. Soon the Master's inner circle increased to twelve, whom he called apostles. There were Peter and his brother Andrew and John and his brother James, who were all fishermen; also called were Philip, Nathaniel, and Matthew along with Thomas, James (son of Alpheus), Thaddaeus, Simon the Cananite, and Judas Iscariot, who betrayed him. Great crowds began following him, bringing their sick and infirmed for healing.

The Passover Festival of the Jews was drawing near, so Jesus and the twelve journeyed to Jerusalem. They traveled the mountain road from Jericho to Jerusalem, the one John had taken so many times. When Jerusalem came into view and they descended the ridge, the young disciple noticed Jesus' rapt awareness of the distant gleaming temple. They entered the great city through the Golden Gate and went directly to the temple. The streets were teeming with Jewish pilgrims from all over Israel and even some from more remote places.

In the precinct of the temple, the Court of the Gentiles, there was much hubbub— the bellowing of cattle, the bleating of sheep, and the cries of merchants trying to attract buyers. Deep resentment and anger showed on Jesus' face as he made a whip of cords. John, always protective, cried out, "Master, please, you will arouse the authorities."

But Jesus began driving the animals out and even overturned the tables of the money changers as he shouted, "How dare you turn my Father's house into a marketplace!"

Some chief priests came out and asked Jesus, "By what authority do you do this? If you have authority, show us a sign."

Jesus answered in an enigmatic way, "Destroy this temple and in three days I will raise it up." They did not understand, but Jesus was speaking of the temple of his body as the disciples later recalled.

John then remembered the scripture: *Zeal for your house will consume me*. He realized that this was the beginning of a sharp break with the Jewish authorities, one which would probably continue until it completely ruptured. He had no idea where all this was leading, but he had complete confidence in his Master.

With great throngs of people already in the city, John was also concerned about finding lodging. He felt they would be welcomed at his uncle's home, especially if Zebedee were not coming, so he excused himself and headed in that direction. Malachi as usual was delighted to see John and did not hesitate to invite Jesus and his disciples into his home.

"Your father is ill, and will not be coming," he told his nephew. Rushing back, John told Jesus and the disciples about the gracious invitation, which they gladly accepted.

As supper was being prepared, John again left and proceeded to the palace of the high priest. With so many dramatic events happening, he really had found no time to think of Deborah, but now, being so close, he wanted to see her again. As usual he had no trouble getting past the guard and to the kitchen. Miriam was preparing the evening meal, but she went to get Deborah, who stepped out of the kitchen door where John was waiting. They dropped the formalities and hugged each other; John spoke excitedly, "Deborah, we have found the Messiah and he has called me to follow him! You should hear him preach, and you should witness the miraculous healings and signs he works. I have been blessed to be a part of it all."

John continued relating the unusual events of the past few weeks, but Deborah interrupted him. "John, I hear bits and pieces of conversation. The high priest and chief priests are wary of this Jesus. They are afraid he might be undermining the religious authority of our nation by stirring up popular support for himself."

"I'm afraid what happened this afternoon will add fuel to the fire," John feared. "Jesus drove the animals and money changers out of the temple."

"Won't you be in danger, John?"

"Well, the temple authorities questioned him, but somehow realized he had made a legitimate point. The marketing activities had become a disgraceful affront to the sanctity of the temple and to our God."

"Oh, John, you might be right, but I fear for you and your Master Jesus."

"I must leave, now, Deborah. Maybe you can keep me informed about the attitude of the high priest."

They hugged again, and John turned and left the palace. Walking back, the cleansing of the temple kept running through his mind, and he wondered what startling events would happen next.

XIII

Past Meets Future, Two Key Conversations

That night after supper, the disciples turned in early after a long day of traveling. Malachi also retired. Jesus and John were still up talking about the day's events when someone knocked at the door. John, greatly puzzled about who could be calling so late, went to find out. A distinguished looking, well dressed Pharisee asked, "Is Jesus staying here?"

John inquired, "Could I ask, Sir, who you are and the reason you seek him?"

"My name is Nicodemus. I have been a member of the council for many years, a teacher of the Jews, and one of their primary theologians. I have heard extraordinary things about this man, and I have come secretly to seek him out and learn from him."

John, sensing the good will of the visitor, asked him in and introduced him to Jesus before leaving the room. Nicodemus opened his remarks with a compliment, "Rabbi, we know that you were sent from God, for no one could work the signs you work apart from God."

The Master quickly recognized that Nicodemus was an outstanding example of Old Testament thinking, that is by virtue of his ancestry and performing all legally required deeds, he would enter the kingdom at the close of the age. That is why Jesus made the following, opening remark, "Very truly, I tell you that no one can enter the kingdom of God without being born again."

Taken aback, Nicodemus replied, "How can a man be born again after he has grown old? Can he enter into his mother's womb and be born a second time?"

"Truly, I tell you that no one can enter the kingdom of God without being born of water and the Spirit. That which is born of the flesh is flesh and that which is born of the Spirit is spirit. The wind blows and you hear it, but you do not know where it comes from or where it goes. So it is with the Spirit."

Nicodemus said to Jesus, "How can all this be?"

"Are you a teacher of Israel and do not know this? If you do not believe what I tell you of earthly things, how can I speak clearly to you of heavenly things? No one has descended from heaven except the Son of Man, and whosoever believes in him will enter the kingdom of God.

"For God so loved the world that he gave his only Son so that everyone who believes in him may not perish but may have eternal life. Indeed, God did not send the Son into the world to condemn the world, but in order that the world might be saved through him. Believe in the Son of Man that you might be saved.

"This is the judgment—the light comes into the world and people must make a choice. Some love darkness more than light because their deeds are evil and they don't want to expose them. Others come to the light because they are not afraid to be exposed. Their deeds are in line with God's will."

John, who was in the adjoining room, could not help overhearing most of the conversation. He was beginning to understand the dichotomy between the Old way and the New.

After the festival was over, Jesus and his disciples expressed their heart felt thanks to Malachi, who had become deeply impressed and captivated by the Lord. They left Judea to journey back to Galilee, and although the disciples objected, Jesus took the western road through Samaria. They came close to a Samaritan city called Sychar and stopped at Jacob's well.

Jesus sat down to rest while the disciples went into the city to buy something to eat. The hour was about midday and the sun was bearing down.

A Samaritan woman came to draw water, and Jesus asked her for a drink. The woman said to Jesus, "How is it that you, a Jew, would ask a Samaritan woman for a drink?"

Jesus replied, "If you knew the gift of God and who it is that is talking to you, *you* would have asked for a drink of living water."

The woman said to him, "You have no bucket to draw with and the well is deep. Where would you get this living water? Are you greater than our father Jacob who gave us this well and his sons watered his flock from it?"

Jesus replied, "Everyone who drinks of this well will get thirsty again and have to come and draw water. Those who drink the water I give will never thirst again. In fact, it will become a spring in them gushing up to eternal life."

She said to him, "Sir, give me this living water that I might never have to draw water again from this well."

Jesus said to her, "Go get your husband and return."

She said, "I have no husband."

"You have spoken truly. You have had five husbands and the one with whom you live is not your husband."

"Sir, you must be a prophet. Our people worship on this mountain, but the Jews say that worship must be done in Jerusalem." In the meanwhile the disciples had returned and were listening to the words of Jesus.

The woman said to him, "I know that the Messiah is coming. He will disclose all things to us."

Jesus answered, "I am he—the one who is talking to you now. Woman, listen to me. The day is coming when those who worship God will worship him neither on this mountain nor in Jerusalem. They will worship him in spirit and in truth, for the Father seeks such to worship him. God is spirit, and those who worship him must do so in spirit and in truth."

The disciples were dismayed to find him talking to a Samaritan and a woman at that. John, having been brought up so strictly in Jewish ways, found these circumstances hard to swallow. But Jesus said to them, "These fields are ready for harvest; we cannot neglect them."

The woman left and quickly returned to the town. She called many people together and said, "I met a Jew at the well. He told me all that I have ever done. Could he be the Messiah?" So the Samaritans went to meet him and asked him to stay with them, which he did for two days.

Later they said to one another, "This man speaks the word of God. He must be the Savior of the world." And they believed in him and his teaching.

Later Andrew was talking to John. "I noticed your negative attitude as we returned to the well."

"It's still hard for me to understand the Master speaking to a Samaritan woman."

"John, I know how you were raised, but we must remember that the Master was sent to save the world, not just the Jewish people. He takes every opportunity, regardless of how it looks, to carry out the will of the Father. Today presented such an opportunity."

"I know you're right, my friend. It's hard for me to change so quickly. I guess I'll have to face many more times like this." More times would come, some of them even harder for John to comprehend.

XIV

Now But Not Yet

During the years of his education in Judaism, John had often questioned the rigid legalism which had become so prevalent among the religious leaders of Israel. That was one reason he had left home—in search of something more: perhaps *truth*, perhaps *ultimate meaning*, or perhaps even *God himself*.

John found himself pondering the teachings of Jesus. The good news of the kingdom of God, eternal life, was constantly on the lips of Jesus. His opening message was, *"The time is fulfilled, and the kingdom of God has come near. Repent and believe in the good news."* This message was received with great joy by most people who were living a bleak and aimless life. Its truth was verified by healings and miracles. But Jewish rulers were suspicious and jealous of their positions of power.

John vividly recalled the Baptist reciting Isaiah:

"The people walking in darkness have seen a

great light; on those living in the land of the shadow of death a light has dawned."

John found that Jesus made his points clear mainly by the use of familiar scenes and objects. He listened as Jesus made great use of parables and metaphors. The Prodigal Son was a favorite of everyone. Jesus had told of a father who had two sons. The older was faithful, loyal, and worked hard each day. The other son grew restless and asked for his inheritance. After receiving it, he went to a faraway country and spent it all in licentious living. He was soon penniless and had to take a very menial job of feeding the swine. He did not have enough to eat and often ate from the food he was feeding the pigs.

Finally he said to himself, "It would be better if I return and work for my father. I will go to him and ask for forgiveness, and perhaps he will give me a job as a hired hand."

When he was returning, his father saw him from afar and ran to him, embraced him and kissed him. He then said to his father, "I have sinned against heaven and before you. I am no longer worthy to be called your son."

But the father told the servants to get him the best cloak, to put a ring on his finger and sandals on his feet. He asked the servants to prepare the fatted calf for a party and said, "My son was dead and is now alive. He was lost but now is found." And they started to celebrate.

John had understood that the parable was describing the love of God, but his thoughts had been drawn to his own father's intractable reaction to his leaving home. One evening, Jesus sat talking with John, who described this dilemma to him. In answer, Jesus had replied, "Your father has not recovered from the disappointment of losing you. He has lived his whole life according to the faith of his fathers. Give him more time to reflect and pray. You also should commit it to prayer. The love of our Father in heaven is so great. Trust him."

John remembered Jesus saying such things as:

"You have heard it said that you shall not murder. Whosoever murders shall be liable to judgment. But I say whosoever is angry with his brother shall be liable to judgment.

"It is in your law that you shall not commit adultery. But I say anyone who looks at a woman lustfully has already committed adultery in his heart.

"You have been taught an eye for an eye and a tooth for a tooth.. But I say to you, do not resist one who is evil. If he should strike you on the right cheek, turn the left to him also.

"The law of Moses states that whoever divorces his wife shall give her a certificate of divorce. But I say to you that whoever divorces his wife except for unfaithfulness makes her an adulteress and he who marries a divorced woman commits adultery.

"You have heard it said that you shall love your neighbor and hate your enemy. But I say to you love your enemies and pray for those who persecute you."

John, trying to take all this in, had replied, "These are difficult sayings, Lord. Who can follow them all and be saved?"

Jesus' answer was, "Those who fail to keep everyone of these commandments can be forgiven if they confess their failure and resolve to live an obedient and righteous life. There is, however, one sin which cannot be forgiven; denying and blaspheming the Holy Spirit of God."

In another talk with Jesus, sitting around the fire after the other disciples had retired, John asked, "Master, how is it that the law has stood for hundreds of years, and yet you came to change it?"

Jesus answered, "John, I have not come to change or abolish the law or the prophets; I have come not to abolish but to fulfill them."

On another occasion John asked Jesus, "Master, why do you prefer to call yourself the *Son of Man*?"

To which Jesus explained, "The book of Daniel is one that is close to my heart. Read there about the *Son of Man*."

Later John read from Daniel:

> *I saw in the night visions, and, behold, one like the Son of Man came with the clouds of heaven, and came to the Ancient of days. And they brought him near before him, And there was given him dominion and glory, and a kingdom, that all people, nations, and languages should serve him; his dominion is an everlasting dominion, which shall not pass away, and his kingdom that which shall not be destroyed.*

One night when John felt especially close to Jesus, he asked, "Master, why did you go off into the desert that day after your baptism?"

Up to this point, Jesus had revealed this to no one, but he said to John, "The Spirit drove me into the desert to be sure I was ready for God's ministry. The desert, solitude, and fasting have a way of clearing one's mind and proving one's convictions as well as being a perfect setting for spiritual insight.

"John, I got more than I expected. I was severely tempted by Satan, the spirit of evil. After many days without food, he appeared to me and said, 'If you are the Son of God, turn these stones into bread.'

"I was so hungry I was sorely tempted, but I answered him

with scripture, *'One does not live by bread alone, but by every word that comes from the mouth of God.'*

"He then offered me all the kingdoms of the world with their riches, splendor, and enticements if I would fall down and worship him."

"How did you answer him, Master?"

"I answered from scripture again, *'Worship the Lord your God and serve him only.'* Next, he quoted scripture asking me to jump off a very high place crying out to God for his angels to bear me up. But I quoted scripture back to him, *'Do not put the Lord your God to the test.'* After this, he gave up and left me alone."

John's months with the Baptist had put him nearer his goal; his following Jesus had both drawn him closer to his quest and at the same time challenged his intellectual and spiritual capacity. John still found it to be one of those "now but not yet" situations. He had not yet taken it all in, but he was getting there. He would continue to follow and learn from his Master. It was an exciting time, full of unpredictable and miraculous events. He greatly appreciated the many times Jesus took him aside to more fully explain the meaning of his teaching.

XV

Miracles And Accusation Of Blasphemy

While still in Galilee, Jesus and the disciples came again to Cana where Jesus had worked his first sign—turning water into wine at the wedding feast. A royal official from Capernaum came up to Jesus and said, "Sir, please come down and heal my son. He is at the point of death."

Jesus replied, "Go, your little boy shall live."

The man believed Jesus and started on his way. As he was traveling, his servants met him and told him his child was alive and well. When he asked at what hour the boy began recovering, they said, "Yesterday the fever left him about one in the afternoon." That was the very hour when Jesus had said to him. "Go, your son shall live." When the official's household found out about it, they all became believers.

A Pentecost festival was approaching. This was a harvest festival but its greater significance was its commemoration of the day when the Ten Commandments were given to Israel. Jesus and the disciples went up to Jerusalem. They passed by the Sheep Gate where there was a pool with five porticoes. Many invalids were lying there in hopes of being healed. When the water was stirred up, it was thought that the first one in the pool would receive a healing. The people believed that an angel came down into the pool at odd intervals and stirred the water.

There was a man lying by the pool who had been crippled for 38 years. Jesus took pity on him and asked him if he wanted to be healed.

"Oh I do, Sir. But when the water is stirred, someone always beats me into the pool."

Jesus instructed him, "Stand up, take your mat and walk." The man stood up, picked up his mat and walked.

There were some Pharisees standing by who asked the man, "Why are you carrying your mat on the Sabbath? Don't you know it is unlawful?"

The man replied, "The Rabbi who healed me told me to take it up and walk."

"Who was the man?"

"I do not know his name." For Jesus had disappeared into the crowd.

Later in the temple he encountered Jesus who told him, "You have been made well. Do not sin anymore and nothing worse will happen to you."

The man went to those Pharisees and told them it was Jesus who had made him well. He also told them that Jesus had said, "I am doing the works of my Father in heaven."

Zebedee, still recovering from his illness, did not make the journey to Jerusalem for Pentecost, so John, Jesus and the other disciples stayed again with Malachi. It was during this visit that Malachi accepted Jesus as Messiah and dedicated his home to the Lord's ministry. That evening before supper, John heard a knock on the door. He opened it to find Deborah standing there, out of breath from her fast pace. He hugged her and she kissed him on the lips as they clung to each other for a few short moments. "John, I had to come quickly and tell you."

"What is it Deborah?"

"The chief priests have met with the high priest in the palace. They plan to bring Jesus' name before the council and charge him with instructing others to break the Sabbath law, and also with blasphemy by claiming to be the Son of God."

"Do you know when the council will meet?"

"I'm not sure but it will probably be sometime tomorrow. I must get back to the palace before I am missed." With that, she told John good night and hurried away.

The next day as Jesus was teaching in the temple, the Jews accosted him, making the same accusations to his face. Jesus answered them candidly, "The Son can do nothing on his own, only what he sees the Father doing. The Father loves the Son and discloses to him all that the Father is doing. You will see much greater works than these, and you will be amazed. Indeed just as the Father gives life to the dead, so the Son will give life to whomever he chooses. Truly I tell you, anyone who hears my words and believes the one who sent me has everlasting life and does not face judgment, but has passed from death to life. For just as the Father has life in himself, so he has given the Son authority to have life in himself. And he has granted him the right to carry out judgment because he is the Son of Man.

"Do not think that I am your accuser. You are already accused because your accuser is Moses on whom you set your hope. If you really believe Moses, you would believe me also, because he wrote about me."

Before the Sanhedrin could meet, Jesus and the disciples left Judea and traveled toward Galilee. When the council met, Caiaphas, the high priest, introduced a motion to indict Jesus on charges of blasphemy. There was a short debate in which Nicodemus stood up for Jesus, requesting that he be given a chance to defend himself. But the Pharisees and chief priests had already made up their minds. The indictment passed.

Jesus resumed his teaching in the synagogues of Galilee and was healing all kinds of diseases. Again large crowds seeking healing and spiritual comfort began to follow him; the months quickly passed. John was able to get home when the company of disciples was in or near Capernaum. He and James visited with Salome, but Zebedee was too sick or ill tempered to see them. John believed that Jesus could heal Zebedee, but the old Jew was too irascible to even consider it. Peter also had a number of visits with his wife, Rachel, whose mother had come to live with her. When he was not in Nazareth, Jesus occasionally stayed with Peter.

One day, Jesus said to his disciples, "Let us cross to the other side of the sea, where we can have a short rest from the crowds." They boarded a boat and made the crossing. However, the large crowds persisted in following him because of the signs he was doing for the sick. Jesus went up on a hillside and sat down with his disciples, but looking up they saw the crowds coming after them.

XVI

The Bread Of Life

Jesus said to Philip, "Where are we to buy enough bread to feed them?" For they were in a desolate and deserted place.

Philip answered him, "Six month's wages would not be enough to buy a little for each one."

Andrew spoke up and said, "There's a little boy here with five barley loaves and two fish, but that won't be enough to feed many people."

Jesus said, "Tell the people to sit down." There was an abundance of grass in the area, so they sat down, about 5000 of them. Jesus then took the loaves and fish, gave thanks, and began to break them up and give them to his disciples to distribute. When the people had eaten their fill, Jesus directed his disciples to pick up the fragments so that nothing would be lost. They filled twelve baskets with the left over pieces.

When the people saw the miracle he had done, they began to exclaim, "Surely this is the prophet who is to come." Jesus realized that they were about to take him by force and make him king, so he withdrew to the mountain by himself. John and Peter, understanding Jesus' motive in leaving, turned back those who tried to follow.

When evening had come, the disciples got into a boat to return to the other side to Capernaum. When they had rowed only a short way, a strong wind suddenly came up against them. The sea became very rough with waves rising to six feet. The disciples made no headway and had to row with all their strength to keep the bow pointed into the wind. Even then an occasional wave would break into the boat gradually filling it with water. When their plight looked desperate, Peter glanced up and saw Jesus walking on the water toward them. They became terrified, thinking he was a ghost, but Jesus said, "It is I. Do not be afraid." Then they took him into the boat, and instantly the boat reached the land where they were going.

The next day, the crowd realized that the disciples had left in the only boat, but without Jesus. When some boats from Tiberias came near, many of them got into the boats and went to Capernaum looking for Jesus. When they found him there, they questioned him, "Rabbi, when did you come here?"

He answered, "Are you looking for me on account of the food you ate? Do not look for perishable food, but for the food that endures to eternal life, which the Son of Man will give to you."

The following Sabbath the Jews asked him, "What must we do to carry out the works of God?"

Jesus answered, "To do the works of God, you must believe in the one whom he sent."

"What sign do you show us that we may believe? Our

fathers ate manna in the wilderness as it is written, "He gave them food from heaven."

Jesus replied, "It was not Moses who gave your ancestors food; it was my Father. He now gives you the true bread which comes down from heaven and gives life to the world."

They asked, "Sir, give us this bread."

Jesus said, "I am the bread of life. Whoever comes to me will never be hungry, and he that believes in me will never thirst. I have come down from heaven to do the will of my Father. And this is his will—that I shall lose nothing of what he has given me, but will raise it up on the last day. Indeed, it is the will of the Father that all who believe in the Son should have eternal life."

The Jews then began to complain among themselves. "Is this man not from Nazareth? Is he not the son of Mary and Joseph? How can he claim that he has come down from heaven?"

Jesus answered, "Everyone who has learned from the Father comes to me. Only the one from God has seen the Father. Very truly, I tell you, whoever believes in me has eternal life. I am that bread of life. Your ancestors ate manna in the wilderness and died. This is the bread that comes down from heaven; those who eat of it shall live forever. I am the living bread which came down from heaven, and the bread which I will give is my flesh which I will give for the life of the world."

Hearing this, the Jews began to question among themselves, "How can this man give us his flesh to eat?"

Jesus said to them, *"Unless you eat the flesh of the Son of Man and drink his blood, you have no life in you. Whoever eats my flesh and drinks my blood has eternal life, and I will raise him up at the last day. For my flesh is real food and my blood is real drink. Whoever eats my flesh and drinks my blood remains in me, and I in him. Just as the living Father sent me and I live because of the Father, so the one who feeds on me will live because of me. This is the bread that came down from heaven. Your forefathers ate manna and died, but he who feeds on this bread will live forever."* Jesus gave this teaching in the synagogue at Capernaum.

When the Jews in the synagogue heard these words they said among themselves, "This is a difficult teaching. Who can accept it? Have we not been taught not to drink even the blood of animals slaughtered for food?"

Jesus knowing what was in their hearts asked, *"Does this offend you? Then what if you were to see the Son of Man ascending to where he was before? It is the spirit that gives life; the flesh is useless. The words that I have spoken to you are spirit and life."* Because of this teaching, many who had followed Jesus turned back, unable to understand and grasp the meaning of his words. So he asked the twelve, "Will you leave also?"

Peter who had understood the metaphorical yet extraordinary spiritual meaning of Jesus' words replied, "Lord, you have the words of eternal life. We have come to the *faith* which you so vividly describe. We believe you are the Christ, the Son of the living God."

John also spoke, "Master, where else would we go. We have *absolute faith* in you."

This was their first real test of faith as disciples. In Jesus' words there was a hint of sacrifice and a forerunning reference to the communion at the last supper, neither of which the disciples could understand at this point. It was also the first of the great metaphorical "I am" teachings. There would be others to follow.

XVII

Daring Return For Booths

Autumn was coming on and with it the Festival of Booths. It was a time of happy celebration of good harvests but specifically commemorated the insecure time of wandering in the wilderness when the Jews lived in makeshift booths. During the festival, booths of palm and willow trees were erected and lived in for several days.

Jesus did not want to go to Judea because of the indictment against him. His brothers, who did not believe in him, urged him to go up to Jerusalem and make himself better known. But he said to them, "I don't believe I will go to this festival for my time has not yet fully come." However, after his brothers had left, Jesus also went, not publicly but in secret.

The Jews were speculating about him as to whether he would dare come to Jerusalem. Some wanted to believe in him; others said that he was deceiving the people. All were afraid to speak openly about him for fear of the religious authorities.

Midway through the festival, Jesus went into the temple and began teaching. People were amazed at his words since they said that he had no formal education. Jesus, knowing what they were thinking, said, "This is not my teaching but that of the One who sent me."

Then he said, "Why are you seeking to kill me?"

Someone in the crowd answered, "Who is trying to kill you? You must have a demon."

Jesus replied, "The patriarchs gave us a law permitting circumcision on the Sabbath, and you do not break that law. And yet I heal a man's whole body on the Sabbath and you are angry with me. Use right, not superficial judgment."

The Jews mumbled among themselves, "Is this not the man the council has indicted? And yet he speaks openly among us." The Pharisees heard the crowd muttering and arguing, so they sent the temple police to restore order and place Jesus under arrest.

But Jesus said, "I will be with you for a little longer, and then I must depart to be with my Father. You will look for me but not find me, for where I am going you cannot come."

There was speculation then among the crowd, "Is he going into the dispersion to teach the Greeks?"

And another said, "What does he mean by saying we cannot follow?"

Then Jesus called out, "Let those who are thirsty come to me, and let him who believes in me drink. As the scripture has said, 'Streams of living water will flow from within him.'" As John came to understand, he was speaking about the Spirit, which had not yet come because Jesus had not been glorified.

There was much debate then among the people. Some said that he was the Messiah. Others said he was the prophet who was to come. Still others doubted him because they said the

Messiah comes from David, from the town of David, Bethlehem.

The temple police went back to the chief priests who asked them, "Why did you not take him into custody?"

They replied, "We have never heard anyone speak as he does. We were enthralled by his words. We do not know who he is."

Jesus and his disciples remained in Jerusalem, and he did much teaching in the temple. He taught them saying, "I am the light of the world. Those who follow me will never walk in darkness but will have the light of life." He said to some who believed in him, "If you commit sin, you are a slave to sin and you will not be free. But if you continue in my word, you are truly my disciples and you will know the truth and the truth shall make you free."

Jesus then told his disciples plainly, "The Son of Man will be rejected by the scribes, Pharisees, and chief priests. He must undergo great suffering at their hands and be killed, but will be raised to life again on the third day." This statement caused great distress among the disciples and was perplexing especially since they could not yet fully understand God's great plan for human redemption.

Late one afternoon a messenger arrived from Capernaum. He had a message for James and John—that their father Zebedee was gravely ill. The brothers talked it over, and it was decided that John would go to Capernaum to check on Zebedee. He and the messenger made rapid time and arrived there early one evening. Salome greeted John with a somber face, but happy as usual to see her younger son. "Your father is very ill; he is calling for you and James."

When John entered Zebedee's bedroom, he was shocked to see his father looking so pale and weak. He walked over to the bed and kissed him on the forehead. Zebedee looked up and made a faint smile. "I'm glad you're here, son. There are many things I need to tell you. First, I hope you will forgive me. I've tried my whole life to live according to the teachings of Moses and those put forward by our rabbis and religious leaders. Second, it's difficult for an old man to change and accept new ways. But in recent weeks I have pored over the books of the prophets. I have earnestly tried to fathom their wisdom. I do believe the Messiah is coming. Finally, I will confess that, according to all I have heard of your Jesus, he might very well be the Anointed One." At this point, Zebedee paused and coughed a number of times.

John replied, "Oh, Father, how I have prayed and ached to have this reconciliation. God be praised! Of course you have my forgiveness and love."

Zebedee continued, "John, I am very old, and I don't believe I'll be here much longer. Please tell me more about your Master."

For the next two hours, John related many of the highlights of Jesus' preaching and healing ministry. The old man hung on every word, and when John paused briefly, he softly said, "Son, you are very persuasive. You must do two things for me. First, give James my love and ask his forgiveness; then tell Jesus that I believe he is doing the work of the Father. I would be grateful for his blessing" At that moment, Salome appeared in the doorway and beckoned for John to let Zebedee rest a while.

After they left the room, John eagerly related the same unique events to Salome. She was sympathetic and eager to believe. When they finished their discussion which lasted well into the night, John was convinced his mother had accepted Jesus as Messiah.

The next morning before John left, he had one more conversation with his father. Zebedee announced that he was writing his will: the house in Capernaum and the fishing business would be left to Salome, while each son would receive a portion of his life savings. Father and son embraced and expressed their love for each other. Zebedee's parting words were, "The Lord go with you, John."

XVIII

The Man Born Blind

Late one night after most of the disciples had retired, John spoke with Jesus, "Master, as you know I just returned from Capernaum."

"I know, John, how is your father?"

"His age has made him weak and frail, but he's had a near miraculous change of heart. He asked for forgiveness and has been studying the prophecies about the coming Messiah. He is most impressed with your words and works and inclined to believe you are the One. And he humbly begs for your blessing."

"May God's peace be with him and may he receive the good news of the kingdom." Jesus then uttered a silent prayer for Zebedee.

John added, "My mother has accepted you and now believes you are the Anointed One."

Jesus replied, "I commend you, John, for your evangelistic

zeal. Sometimes one's family is the most difficult to win over, and I thank the Father for drawing her near and speaking to your father through the scriptures."

Several weeks went by with the chief priests hesitating to arrest Jesus because of his popularity with the people. Each day he taught in the temple, and one day the scribes and Pharisees brought a woman to him. They said, "Teacher, this woman was caught in the act of adultery. Moses commanded that such women be stoned. What do you say?"

Jesus bent down and wrote on the ground with his finger. When they continued to question him, he straightened up and said, "Let him who has no sin cast the first stone." He then bent down and continued to write. One by one starting with the elders the Jews walked away. Jesus again straightened up and asked the woman, "Is there no one left to condemn you?"

She answered, "No one, Sir."

Jesus replied, "I don't condemn you either. Go, and sin no more."

Jesus' teaching in the temple that he was the light of the world was the prelude to one of the profound miracles of the Lord.

One Sabbath morning as Jesus was walking to the temple, he came upon a man born blind. His disciples asked him, "Master, who sinned to cause this man to be born blind? Was it he or his parents?

Jesus answered, "It was neither. He was born blind so that the works of my Father might be revealed. While I am in the world, I am the light of the world." Having said that he bent over, spat upon the ground and made some mud. He then spread the mud over the man's eyes.

After that, he instructed him, "Go wash your eyes in the pool of Siloam." The man obeyed and came back able to see. This miracle caused quite a stir among the people who had known the man as a beggar.

Some said, "Is not this the blind man who used to sit here and beg?"

Others said, "It is not the same man, but he does resemble him."

The beggar kept saying to them, "I am the man." They then asked him how it was that he could now see. He told them what Jesus had done and how he had opened his eyes.

They asked, "Where is Jesus now?" He answered, "I do not know."

They brought the formerly blind man to the Pharisees who asked him, "Were you born blind?"

"I was," he replied.

"Then how is it that you can now see?"

"The man named Jesus put mud on my eyes and told me to wash it off. I did so, and now I can see."

"This man Jesus is not from God for he breaks the law of the Sabbath," a Pharisee exclaimed.

"Then how can a sinner open the eyes of the blind?" another asked.

A debate then took place with the Pharisees divided. One of them asked the beggar, "It was your eyes that he opened. What do you think about him?"

"I was blind, but now I see; he is a prophet."

Most of the Jews did not believe the man had been born blind, so they called for his parents who gave testimony that the man was indeed their son, and that he had been born blind. But when questioned further (in fear that they might be thrown out of the synagogue) they said, "Ask him. He is of age. He will tell you."

They brought the beggar back in and asked him again, "How is it that you can see?"

Exasperated, he said, "I have told you once and you would not listen. Why do you want to hear it again? Are you interested in becoming his disciples?"

Upon hearing this, the Pharisees reviled him, "We are disciples of Moses. This man is a sinner."

"Now, isn't this amazing," he replied. "You don't know this man and yet you say he is a sinner. God doesn't listen to sinners, and still this man opened my eyes." The sarcasm of his statement angered the Jews, who insulted and heaped scorn upon the man, driving him out of the temple.

It was evident to John that this episode plainly delineated the difference between the legalistic Pharisees, who believed their spiritual leader was Moses, and the followers of Jesus who believed he was the Son of God. It also showed John the extremes the Pharisees would go to in trying to discredit the miracles of Jesus. The young disciple felt it was a foreboding of the conflicts to come.

XIX

Good Shepherd & Lazarus

One day as Jesus was teaching in the temple, he exclaimed, *"I am the good shepherd. The good shepherd lays down his life for the sheep. The hired hand is not the shepherd who owns the sheep. So when he sees the wolf coming, he abandons the sheep and runs away. Then the wolf attacks the flock and scatters it. The man runs away because he is a hired hand and cares nothing for the sheep.*

"I am the good shepherd; I know my sheep and my sheep know me—just as the Father knows me and I know the Father—and I lay down my life for the sheep. I have other sheep that are not of this sheep pen. I must bring them also. They too will listen to my voice, and there shall be one flock and one shepherd. The reason my Father loves me is that I lay down my life—only to take it up again. No one takes it from me, but I lay it down on my own accord. I have authority to lay it down and

authority to take it up again. This command I received from my Father." These last statements surprised and puzzled John.

The months quickly went by and soon it was winter. Hanukkah was approaching, and Jesus, accompanied by Peter, James, and John, was walking in the temple in the portico of Soloman. The Jews approached him and gathered around him. "Tell us, are you the Messiah?"

He answered, "I have told you and you do not believe me. You have seen my works, and still you do not believe me because you are not of my sheep. They hear my voice and will follow me, and I will give them eternal life. No one will take them from me, and no one can snatch them out of my Father's hand. I am in the Father and the Father is in me."

Hearing this, they wanted to stone him for blasphemy. The temple police again tried to arrest him, but he slipped out of their hands and disappeared into the crowd.

After this, Jesus and his disciples went across the Jordan to the place where John the Baptist had been baptizing earlier, and they stayed there for several weeks. Large numbers came to Jesus and believed in him. Although the Baptist had performed no miracles, his memory was still very much alive in the minds of the people, and they recalled that everything he had said about Jesus was true.

The Baptist had criticized King Herod for taking the wife of his own brother in marriage. But it was most probable that Herod was afraid of John's great following and had imprisoned him out of fear of an uprising. The Baptist was executed in

Herod's palace, and the event kept secret for sometime. John remembered the day Jesus heard about the execution and how he had said, "Among mortals there was no greater man than John. He went before me to prepare the way. He will be remembered as outstanding among the prophets."

John Bar Zebedee had a very heavy heart. He had left Deborah without saying goodbye, and he was still mourning the death of John the Baptist. The Baptist had exercised a profound spiritual influence upon him, one he would never forget. His companionship at a critical time in John's life was especially reassuring and supportive. He was deeply saddened by the loss of the Prophet—his mentor and friend. But when depressed by these thoughts, John was encouraged by the great privilege of being chosen to follow Jesus.

John recalled in vivid detail the mountain top experience when Jesus asked him, Peter and James to accompany him. They had climbed to the summit of the mountain. Suddenly the garments Jesus was wearing turned dazzling white, and his face shone like the sun; two men were seen talking to him. When Jesus addressed them, it became evident that they were Moses and Elijah. The three of them discussed the coming crisis in Jerusalem and the glorification of the Son of God.

Peter, overwhelmed and a little irrational, had offered to make three booths, one each for Jesus, Elijah and Moses. About that time, a cloud covered them and when it disappeared the disciples saw only Jesus standing there, his appearance normal. If there had been any doubt about Jesus' identity, this spectacular event had erased it....

"John...John," a voice was calling him, arousing him out of his daydream. It was Peter who said, "Brother, you must have been in another world. Jesus has just received a message that Lazarus, his good friend, is very ill. I don't understand the Master, for he said we will stay here for two more days."

"Well, you know, Peter. He has the amazing ability of knowing what is going on many miles away. I'm sure he has good reasons for such a decision."

After two days, Jesus said to his disciples, "Come, let us go to Judea again."

John replied, "Master, the Jews were just trying to arrest or kill you. Are you going there again?"

Jesus responded, "Are there not twelve hours of daylight? Those who walk in the day do not stumble because they have the light of this world. Those who walk in darkness will stumble because the light is not in them. Our friend Lazarus has fallen asleep. I go to awaken him."

Peter answered, "If he is asleep, will he not recover when he awakens?"

Jesus told them plainly, "Lazarus has died. But for your sake and the sake of all who are there, this will be an occasion to show forth the glory of God—so that all may believe."

It was a two day journey from Bethany across the Jordan to Bethany near Jerusalem. Many Jews had come from Jerusalem to console Martha and Mary who were sisters of the dead man. When Martha heard that Jesus was coming, she ran to meet him. She embraced him and sobbed, "Lord if only you had been here, my brother would not have died, but even now I know that God will listen to anything you ask of him."

Jesus said, "Your brother will rise again."

"I know he will rise at the resurrection on the last day," she agreed.

Jesus replied, "I am the resurrection and the life. All who believe in me, though they die, they will live forever. Do you believe this?"

Martha answered, "Lord, I believe you are the Christ, the Son of God, who is coming into the world."

When she had said this, she went into the house and called Mary, "The Master is here; he is calling for you." Mary got up immediately and went to meet Jesus. The Jews from Jerusalem, thinking that Mary was going to the grave to mourn, followed her out.

When Mary approached Jesus, she fell at his feet and cried, "Lord, you could have kept him from dying."

Seeing Mary as well as all the Jews weeping, Jesus was greatly disturbed in spirit and wept. He asked, "Where have you laid him?"

They replied, "Come and see."

They took Jesus to a cave with a great stone rolled over the entrance. Jesus ordered, "Take away the stone."

"But Lord," Martha complained, "he has been dead for four days and there will be a stench."

But Jesus answered, "Haven't I told you that if you believed, you would witness the glory of God?"

They rolled away the stone and Jesus prayed, "Father, I am thankful that you have heard me. You always hear me, but I am saying this so that all standing here might believe that you sent me."

Jesus then cried out in a loud voice, "Lazarus, come out." The man who had been dead for four days came out, his body bound with grave clothes and his face wrapped in a cloth. Jesus commanded, "Unbind him and let him go."

The Jews who had come from Jerusalem spread the word quickly when they returned. As soon as the scribes and Pharisees heard it, they called a meeting of the council and asked each other, "What are we to do. This man, Jesus, is performing many signs, which are attracting great numbers of people. If we let this go on, the Romans will come and destroy our nation and our holy places."

Then the high priest Caiaphas stood up. "Don't you understand? It is better that one man should die for the nation rather than the whole nation be destroyed." He did not of course realize it, but he was prophesying the great redemption by Jesus though not for the Jewish nation only, but for the whole world.

From that moment on, the religious rulers of the Jews sought to find Jesus in order to put him to death. They also sought to kill Lazarus since it was because of him that so many people were deserting them and going over to Jesus.

XX

The Last Supper & Betrayal

Now the Passover festival of the Jews was near. Jesus sent Peter and John into Jerusalem to engage a room for the twelve and himself and to prepare the Passover meal. He also asked two disciples to bring him a donkey's colt, which they did with the consent of the owner. Jerusalem, full of pilgrims, was buzzing with excitement about Jesus. Word about the raising of Lazarus had stirred the people to a fever pitch. When Jesus rode into the city, people lined the road and placed branches of palms down before him. They shouted, "Blessed is the one who comes in the name of the Lord—the king of Israel! Hosanna in the highest!"

The scene made the disciples almost ecstatic, and some recalled Zechariah's prophecy:

Rejoice greatly, O daughter of Zion!

Shout aloud, O daughter of Jerusalem!
Lo, your king comes to you;
triumphant and victorious is he,
humble and riding on a donkey,
on a colt, the foal of a donkey.

At supper that night, Jesus took a loaf of bread and after blessing it, he broke it and gave it to his disciples saying, "Take and eat. This is my body." Then he took a cup and after blessing it he said, "This is my blood poured out for many for the remission of sins. Drink from it, all of you. I shall not drink from it again until I drink from it in my Father's kingdom."

After supper, Jesus got up from the table, took off his outer garment and tied a towel around his waist. He took a basin of water and began washing the disciples' feet and drying them with the towel.

When he got to Peter, the big fisherman said, "Lord you will never wash my feet."

Jesus replied, "If I don't wash your feet, you will have no part in me."

Peter said, "Lord, not only my feet, but my hands and my head."

Jesus said to him, "One who has bathed has no need to wash again except for his feet. You are clean, all but one of you." For he knew who would betray him.

When he finished washing the disciples' feet, he put his robe back on, returned to the table and said, "Do you understand what I have done? You call me Master and Lord for that is what I am. If I, your Lord and Teacher, wash your feet, you should do the same for each other. I have set an example for you. If you do these things you will be blessed."

Then Jesus became very troubled and said to them, "One of you will betray me." The disciples looked at each other not knowing of whom he was speaking. John was reclining next to Jesus, and Peter motioned for him to ask who the betrayer was.

So John said to Jesus, "Lord, who is it?"

Jesus answered softly, "It is the one to whom I shall give this bread after I have dipped it into the dish." He dipped the bread and gave it to Judas and said, "Do what you are going to do quickly." Satan came into Judas and he departed. The other disciples had not heard Jesus and thought that he had told Judas to buy what was needed for the festival.

After Judas had left, Jesus again addressed the disciples, "God has been glorified in the Son and God will also glorify the Son in himself. My hour has come, and I give you a new commandment—you should love each other as I have loved you. John wondered how anyone could love as Jesus had loved, yet the Master was asking it of the disciples.

"My children, I will be with you for only a short time longer. As I have told the Jews, 'Where I am going, you cannot follow.'"

Peter asked, "Lord, why can't I follow you? I will lay down my life for you."

Jesus replied, "You will have denied me three times before the cock crows twice."

Jesus continued, "Let not your hearts be troubled. I came into the world from the Father, and I am leaving this world to return to the Father. I am going to prepare a place for you. In my father's house are many dwelling places, and you know the way to the place I am going."

Thomas said to him, "Lord, we do not know where you are going. How can we know the way?"

Jesus answered, "I am the way and the truth and the life. No one comes to the Father except through me. The hour is coming when you will be scattered and leave me alone. The Father is with me so I am not really alone. I have said this to you so you will not be troubled, but have peace. In the world you will face persecution, but take heart, I have overcome the world."

This last conversation with Jesus lasted well into the night with the Master revealing and reviewing many important principles and instructions. John especially remembered that Jesus said, "I am in the Father and the Father is in me. I will not leave you comfortless. Those who love me will be loved by my Father, and I will love them and reveal myself to them."

Jesus then used the metaphor of the vine. "I am the vine and my Father is the vinegrower. If a branch bears no fruit, the Father removes it. As the branch cannot bear fruit unless it abides in the vine, so you can do nothing unless you abide in me. Whoever does not abide in me is thrown away and withers. These branches are picked up and thrown into the fire and burned.

"The Father will send the Holy Spirit to you, and he will teach you everything and remind you of all I have taught you. Peace I leave with you, my peace I give to you, not as the world gives. Again I say to you, do not let your hearts be troubled. Come, arise, let us be going."

They walked across the Kidron valley to a walled garden, where they had met many times. Jesus then prayed for the disciples. "Father, protect them in your name. When I was with them I protected them in your name so they may be one as we are one. The glory you gave me, I have given them. I guarded them, and not one of them was lost except the one destined to betray me so that the scripture might be fulfilled. Sanctify them in the truth, your word is truth. I do not ask you to take them out of the world, but to protect them from the evil one. As you sent me into the world, so I send them."

The religious authorities had waited to seek the right moment to arrest Jesus. They were afraid of the great masses of people who had welcomed and praised him upon his entry.

They needed to find and arrest him by night, convict him, and humiliate him. They needed to do it quickly before the people could react. Judas was the key, and had made it known that he was willing to betray Jesus for a price.

Satan was working in Judas, telling him that Jesus was not the hero he expected, telling him that Jesus was not going to offer himself as king and drive the Romans out of Israel. He was even putting into Judas's mind that somehow Jesus had to be provoked into taking on the personality of an avenging warrior. Perhaps his attempted arrest would do just that. Being so driven, Judas had taken 30 pieces of silver from the chief priests in order to lead them to Jesus by night. This contorted scheme made little sense, but Judas, who had opened his mind to Satan, was driven by his demons to believe it.

As Jesus was praying for the disciples, John had stationed himself near the opening in the garden wall. He thought he saw a flash of light. Then it grew brighter and he could make out a large number of figures bearing lanterns and torches and coming in their direction.

XXI

Arrest And Trial

John could plainly see them now—Judas was leading a detachment of soldiers and temple police armed with swords and clubs toward the garden. John felt a sudden pang of fear in the pit of his stomach as he hastened to tell Jesus. His Master, however, calmly walked to the entrance and faced the throng.

"Whom are you looking for?" he asked.

"Jesus of Nazareth," shouted one of the men.

"I am he," Jesus replied.

Instantly the whole group stepped back and fell to the ground.

When they recovered, Jesus said, "I told you, I am he, so if you are looking for me, let these men go." The disciples fled in fear, fulfilling Zechariah's prophesy:

> *Strike the shepherd*
> *and the sheep will be scattered...*

John fled with the rest and somehow they all became separated in the dark. He felt ashamed and angry, but fear drove him on. Finally, coming to a road, he hid in a small grove of trees along the side and remained there for a few moments. The more he considered his actions, the more ashamed he became. Finally he gathered up enough nerve to return to Jerusalem. At this late hour, he thought, the most probable place they would take his Master was the palace of the high priest. Once in Jerusalem, he approached the palace gate cautiously. A large man was lurking just inside the shadows.

"Is that you, John?" Peter whispered. The two friends embraced each other.

"How did you get here?" John asked.

"I followed the Lord and his captors at a distance, but I'm afraid I won't be able to get past the gate."

"Wait here until I check things out. If I get in, you can perhaps follow."

John walked toward the house and came to the courtyard gate. A young woman was just inside. Could it be...? It was Deborah. John took a deep breath of relief and called to her. She unlocked the gate and said in a panicky voice, "John, they have taken your Master into the large room, where the chief priests, and some scribes and Pharisees are gathered. I fear for his life."

John replied, "It seems most of the temple police are in the courtyard. Maybe I can get into the house close enough to hear what's going on. Let my friend, Peter, in the gate."

"Please be careful," she whispered.

He strode across the courtyard as if he were expected and almost made it to the door when a guard spotted him. "Halt, Galilean! What are you doing here?"

John's heart sank. He had no ready excuse, so two large guards grabbed him and hustled him back to the gate. As they threw him to the ground outside, one shouted, "Come back and you'll be arrested." There was nothing Deborah could do; John pulled himself up and moved away into the shadows.

Deborah had let Peter inside the courtyard, and at first unnoticed, he sat by the fire with others who were warming themselves. But one of the other servant girls passed by and said to him, "You also followed Jesus, didn't you?"

Peter answered, "I don't know the man," and he walked away from the fire and the cock crowed.

The servant girl persisted in following him and said to the bystanders, "This man is indeed one of them." But Peter denied it again.

Then one of the guards said, "Weren't you with him in the garden?" Then Peter began to curse and swear that he did not know Jesus. At that moment the cock crowed again and Peter remembered what Jesus had said, and swiftly leaving the courtyard, he broke down anc cried bitterly.

When the mock trial ended, the scribes, priests and some Pharisees began leaving the courtyard. Looking on from the darkness, John finally recognized Nicodemus. He pulled the Pharisee into the shadows and pleaded to know what had taken place. It was evident Nicodemus had been highly agitated, but he calmed down enough to relate the essence of the trial.

He began, "The high priest asked for testimony against Jesus. Many voices spoke, but none of them agreed. One even exclaimed, 'Jesus said he would destroy this temple made with hands and in three days would build it back without hands.' But even on this they could not agree.

"Finally the high priest addressed Jesus, 'Tell us, are you the Messiah?'

"Jesus answered, 'I am, and you will see the Son of Man seated at the right hand of Power and coming on the clouds of heaven.'

"Then the high priest angrily declared, 'You have heard this blasphemy. We need no more! What is your decision?'

"With my one exception, they all voted to condemn Jesus to death. Afterward, some came to spit on him, while others blindfolded him, struck him on the face and demanded, 'Prophesy! Who was that who struck you?' When I saw Jesus being humiliated, I strongly protested, but I was held back and escorted to the door. As I left I could hear the guards also beginning to abuse him."

When John heard this, he burned with anger, and he remembered the Baptist quoting the Suffering Servant songs, *"I hid not my face from shame and spitting."*

He asked Nicodemus, "What can we do? Where will they take him?"

The Pharisee replied, "I'm afraid there is nothing we can do. The high priest has called a meeting of the whole Sanhedrin for early in the morning. Jesus will be brought there."

Disconsolate, John returned to the Malachi house, but he could not sleep. He arose very early and went to the temple. He knew the Sanhedrin would meet there in their chambers. When the whole council met to ratify the midnight trial at the high priest's palace, no one defended Jesus except Nicodemus and Joseph of Arimathea, and they were shouted down and vilified. The mock trial had accomplished the high priest's purpose.

Now the council had a problem. It was unlawful for them to officially put a person to death, although a few stonings had taken place. They wanted the Romans to carry out the sentence for two reasons. Any sympathizers would be intimidated, and more importantly they wanted Jesus crucified. This Roman method of execution would be the most humiliating since the Jewish scripture stated, *"... for anyone hung on a tree is under God's curse."*(The scripture actually applied to murderers and the worst convicted criminals.) So they bound Jesus and took him to Pilate, the Roman governor.

John did not hear what took place in the council chambers, but he had already heard enough. He knew the council would overwhelmingly endorse the mock trial at the palace. So he followed the group who took Jesus to Pilate. The chief priests had assembled some rabble and other bystanders to support their demand. Staying near the back, John followed the mob.

Pilate was an intelligent man who tried his best to balance the wishes of the Jews with a strict Roman rule. His major task was to keep the peace and prevent any uprising. In order to avoid ritual defilement, the Jews did not go into Pilate's headquarters, so Pilate came out and asked, "What charge do you make against this man?"

The Jews answered, "If he were not a criminal, we would not have brought him to you."

Pilate returned into his headquarters and ordered Jesus to be brought in. He asked, "Are you the king of the Jews?"

Jesus answered, "Do you ask this or did someone else tell you to ask?"

Pilate said, "I am not a Jew. Your own people have handed you over to me. Tell me what you have done?"

Jesus replied, "My kingdom is not of this world. If it were, I would have many defending me."

"So you claim to be a king?" Pilate asked.

"You say that I am a king," Jesus said, "the reason I came into the world was to testify to the truth."

"What is truth?" Pilate cynically asked.

After this interrogation, Pilate went out to the Jews again. "I find no case against this man." Thinking that he might solve the problem without further antagonism, Pilate offered, "At this time each year, we release one prisoner to you. Which would you have me release, Jesus or Barabbas?" (Now, Barabbas was a bandit and a conspirator.)

The mob shouted, "Barabbas. Release Barabbas!"

Then Pilate ordered that Jesus be flogged. This punishment was expected to draw a confession out of the victim.

The soldiers took off Jesus' outer garments and tied him to a post. A brawny Roman soldier took up a whip consisting of several leather thongs fitted with pieces of metal on the ends. He began flailing Jesus. The metal shredded Jesus' flesh causing severe pain and bleeding. The scourging continued until the soldier grew tired, but the torture did not stop. The soldiers wove a crown of thorns and put it on his head, dressed him in a purple robe, and humiliated him further by hailing him as king of the Jews and repeatedly striking him on the face. This fulfilled the prophecy of Isaiah about his suffering:

> *Just as there were many who were astonished at him—so marred was his appearance, beyond human semblance, and his form beyond that of mortals....*

Finally, Pilate brought Jesus out again, thinking that his pitiable condition might cause the Jews to relent and be satisfied. He pronounced, "This is the man. I can find no case against him."

But the Jews cried, "Crucify him! Crucify him!"

At this point Pilate became frustrated with the whole spectacle and said, "Take him and crucify him yourselves."

One of the chief priests shouted, "He claimed to be king, but we have no king but Caesar. If you release him you are no friend of Caesar's." Then Pilate, fearful of Caesar's displeasure and tired of pleading with the Jewish mob, turned Jesus over to them to be crucified.

A dizzying complexity of emotions gripped John—fierce anger at the chief priests, futility at his own helplessness, and acute grief for his Master. His grief broke into sobs as he shuddered to think of what was coming next.

XXII

Crucifixion & Resurrection

John's head was light and spinning. On the way to the place of crucifixion, he saw Jesus walking between two Roman soldiers and carrying the heavy cross piece of roughly hewn wood. The Lord's bruised and battered condition had drained the strength from his frame and he fell to the ground. One of the soldiers commandeered a bystander to carry the cross piece, pulled Jesus up by his hair and shoved him forward.

The chief priests knew the procession would wind through several streets before departing the gates of the city. They wanted the people to see Jesus in this pitiable condition. Leaving the city, the group mounted a small hill just outside. This was commonly a place of crucifixion, the upright poles already being in place. Jesus was stretched out upon the ground with the crosspiece under his shoulders. His hands were then nailed to the timber with large spikes just above the wrists. The impact of each spike sent an electric-like shock through Jesus' body. As his blood covered the ground, he exclaimed, "Father, forgive them, for they know not what they do."

He was then hoisted up the standing timber. The crosspiece was raised to the slot and secured to the upright, and the feet of Jesus nailed below, one above the other. Blood flowing from his feet seeped down the upright, staining it red again. Two criminals were also crucified, one on his right and the other on his left.

The Romans adopted crucifixion from other civilizations, but then perfected it and used it extensively. One of its special features was to show the public what would happen to those who opposed Roman rule. The humiliating and long, painful display was calculated to ward off further would-be conspirators. The ordeal could last for days ending in suffocation when the victim could no longer push up on his feet.

The Roman soldiers divided Jesus' clothes into four parts, one part for each soldier. The piece left over was the tunic which was seamless, woven in one piece. They decided to cast lots for it, for this was to fulfill the prophecy in Psalm 22:

> *They divided my clothes among themselves,*
> *and for my clothing they cast lots.*

There was an inscription placed above Jesus' head which read: Jesus of Nazareth, King of the Jews. It was written in Hebrew, Greek, and Latin. The chief priests had objected, asking Pilate to change it to, "This man said I am King of the Jews." But Pilate had experienced enough of the brazenness of the Jewish hierarchy, and he let the inscription stand.

Jesus was taunted by the chief priests and some of the scribes and elders who walked by. One shouted, "You saved others, but you cannot save yourself."

Others cried out, "You who said you would destroy the temple and build it back in three days, save yourself."

Another shouted, "You claimed to be the Son of God, call on God to save you."

One of the criminals also derided him saying, "If you are the Messiah, save yourself and us!"

But the other rebuked him, saying, "Do you not fear God? We are under the same condemnation and have been condemned justly, but this man is innocent." And he turned to Jesus and said, "Remember me, Jesus, when you come into your kingdom."

Jesus replied, "You will soon be with me in Paradise."

John stood there with Mary, the mother of Jesus, her sister, and Mary Magdalene. When Jesus saw his mother standing there with John, he said, "Woman, here is your son." And to his beloved disciple, he said, "here is your mother." John immediately decided to take Mary into the Malachi home.

Several hours went by with Jesus suffering unbearable pain and gasping for breath From noon until three in the afternoon darkness came over the whole land. When Jesus knew that all was accomplished, he said, "I thirst." A jar of sour wine was standing there, so one of the soldiers put a sponge filled with the wine on a branch of hyssop and held it to his mouth. When Jesus had received the wine he said, "It is finished!" And he bowed his head and gave up his spirit. The Son of God had suffered the very worst that mankind could inflict upon him.

As the Sabbath was quickly approaching, the Jews wanted the bodies removed from the crosses, especially since that Sabbath during Passover was an important festival. To speed death, the soldiers broke the legs of the two bandits, but when they approached Jesus they saw that he was dead. Just to be sure, one of them thrust his spear through the Lord's side. Blood and water poured out. These things occurred so that the scripture in Psalm 34 might be fulfilled:

> *He protects all his bones; not one of them will be broken.*

And in Zechariah:

> *They will look upon the one they have pierced.*

Joseph of Arimathea, a wealthy man who had been a disciple of Jesus, went to Pilate and requested the Master's body. His request was granted, so he took the body down to prepare it for burial. Nicodemus, who had come by night to talk to the Lord, brought about a hundred pounds of myrrh and aloes to assist with the burial. They wrapped the body of Jesus with spices and linen cloths according to the custom of the Jews. There was a garden nearby which had a new tomb in which no one had been buried, and because it was the Jewish day of Preparation, they laid the body of Jesus there.

Early on the morning of the first day of the week, Mary Magdalene came to the tomb and found the stone rolled away. Frightened and alarmed, she ran to Simon Peter who was with John and said, "Someone has rolled the stone away from the tomb. I fear someone has taken the body of the Lord away." The two men raced to the tomb, but John being the youngest arrived before Peter. He peered into the tomb and saw the linen wrappings lying there, but he did not enter. Peter reached the tomb a moment later and went in. He saw the linen wrappings lying as if the body had simply vanished. The head cloth was folded neatly in a different place. John then entered the tomb, and as he instantly recalled the many times Jesus had foretold his rising, *he believed*. The two disciples left with great expectations and returned to the Malachi house.

But Mary returned and found it difficult to leave the tomb. When she looked in, she saw two men dressed in white sitting where the body of Jesus had lain. They asked, "Woman, why are you weeping?"

She answered, "They have taken away my Lord's body." Then sensing another presence behind her, she turned and saw Jesus standing there; but in her sorrow and tears, she didn't recognize him until he said, "Mary."

Instantly she recognized his voice and trembling with astonishment cried, "Rabbouni"(which means Teacher).

He said to her, "Do not hold me, for as yet I have not returned to my Father. But go tell my disciples that I am ascending to my Father and your Father, to my God and your God."

She went and told the disciples, "I have seen the Lord." And she told them what he had said to her. Their hope, joy and confidence began to build.

XXIII

The Appearances

That same night the disciples met in the house where they had shared the last supper. The doors were locked for fear of the Jews, but Jesus came and stood in their midst. He said, "Peace be with you." He showed them the scars where spikes had been driven through his hands and feet and where the spear had pierced his side. The disciples were overjoyed and praised God with loud acclamations and worshipped Jesus. Again Jesus said, "Peace be with you. As the Father has sent me, so I send you."

John, the first disciple to believe, could hardly contain his joy and excitement. Thomas had not been at that first meeting, and when told about Jesus, he would not believe. A week later the disciples met in the same house with locked doors. Jesus again came and stood in their midst and said, "Peace be with you." Then he told Thomas to put his hand in the scars.

Thomas exclaimed, "My Lord and my God!"

Jesus said, "Have you believed because you have seen? Blessed are they who have not seen and yet believe." And he disappeared from their presence.

After the frenetic and momentous events of Passover week, the disciples decided to go back to their homes for a short rest before returning to follow the commission of Jesus. The Galileans journeyed back to the peace and serenity of Galilee. They all agreed to return to Judea and meet on the Mount of Olives one week before Pentecost. John left Mary with faithful friends in the Malachi house, and after telling Deborah goodbye, departed for Galilee.

One afternoon John and Peter were sitting on the beach of the Sea of Galilee reminiscing about the miraculous events of Passover when suddenly Peter exclaimed, "Let's go fishing!" They rounded up James, Andrew, Thomas, Nathanael and Philip and shoved off from shore about sundown. It was one of those beautiful Galilean nights—a slight breeze with small waves lapping at the side of the boat. The sky was clear with a bright half moon and a canopy of glittering stars. Although they fished all night, immensely enjoying the camaraderie and the hard physical exercise, they caught no fish.

Approaching shore at first light, John noticed a lone figure on the beach who called out to them, "Children, have you caught any fish?"

They answered. "No."

"Cast the net on the right side of the boat and you will find some," the man replied.

John picked up the largest cast net aboard and made a cast to the right side. The net opened in a perfect large circle and fell into the sea. When John jerked the net tight and tried to pull it in, the weight was so great he had to call for help. Even then, the men could not lift it into the boat for it was filled with large fish. Sensing the miraculous nature of the catch, John looked again at the man on the shore.

"It is the Lord!" he exclaimed.

Peter who was stripped for fishing, put on his outer garment, jumped into the water and swam rapidly to shore. The other disciples came in the boat dragging the net full of fish.

Jesus said, "Bring some of the fish you have just caught." Simon Peter went aboard and dragged the net filled with large fish ashore. There was a charcoal fire burning with fish and bread on the grill.

"Come and have breakfast," Jesus said to them. The disciples cleaned some of the fish just caught and placed them on the grill. When the fish were cooked, Jesus gave thanks to the Father and passed the fish and bread to each disciple.

Jesus knew that Peter needed forgiveness and confidence following his three denials. And so after breakfast he said to him, "Peter, do you love me more than these?"

Peter replied, "Lord, you know that I love you."

The Lord said, "Feed my lambs."

Then the Lord asked him the second time, "Peter, do you love me?"

"Why yes, Lord, you know I love you."

Jesus said, "Tend my sheep."

Even a third time Jesus asked him, "Do you love me?"

Beginning to get a little frustrated, Peter responded, "You know everything, Lord, and you know that I love you."

"Feed my sheep. When you were young you would fasten your belt and go where you pleased. But when you get old, someone will fasten a belt around you and take you where you do not want to go." (Jesus said this to indicate what kind of death he would experience, glorifying the Lord.) And then Jesus said to Peter, "Follow me."

The two walked down the beach, but Peter turned and saw John following. He said, "Lord, what about John?"

Jesus replied, "If it is my will that he should stay until I return, what is that to you? Follow me." (He did not say that John *would* remain that long, but indicated *if* to show that his will for John might be different from that of Peter's. Indeed, future events would prove this to be the case.)

Pentecost was less than four weeks away, and the disciples wondered what was in store for them. After such spectacular events, what else could it possibly be?

PART III

John And The Spirit

XXIV

Power

Zebedee had rallied following the meeting with John and Jesus' blessing, and he enjoyed good health for several months. But again his age began to plague him with one problem after another. Because of the severity of Zebedee's condition, Malachi had been summoned to Caperanum. The two brothers had several extended conversations about Jesus.

One day while the disciples were still in Galilee, Zebedee called James and John to his side and gave them his blessing. He also confessed that after more scripture searching, news of Jesus, and encouragement from Salome and Malachi, he had accepted Jesus as Lord. He reminded them of the good life he had been blessed with, and indicated he thought his time was drawing near. The young men were saddened by the thought of his departure, but happy about his change of heart and acceptance of Jesus. Two days later Zebedee, the affluent and successful Galilean fisherman, passed away. His funeral was attended by several hundred people from the northwestern corner of the Sea of Galilee.

The seven disciples made plans to return to Jerusalem where they would meet the other four. John and James, after helping Salome sell the business, discussed taking her to Jerusalem. Together with their mother, they decided to rent the house in Capernaum with Salome moving to Jerusalem, where she would live in the Malachi home. She would have the companionship of Mary the mother of Jesus, Zebedee's brother and other faithful followers of the Lord.

When all eleven disciples arrived in Jerusalem, they met together, as planned, on the Mount of Olives. Jesus came again and stood in their midst. He instructed them not to leave Jerusalem until they had received the power of the Spirit. He said, "My Father has given me all authority in heaven and on earth. Go and make disciples of all nations and baptize them in the name of the Father, the Son, and the Holy Spirit, and teach them to obey all things I have commanded you. And remember, I am always with you even until the end of the age." And he was taken up and out of their sight by a cloud.

It was decided that for as long as possible they would meet in the upper room. In their first meeting after the ascension, they determined to accept Matthias to replace Judas Iscariot.

On the day of Pentecost, the disciples were all sitting in the upper room, praying and meditating about the promise of the Lord. John was at peace; he was beginning to understand why Jesus had to die and rise again. The world was sinful—pride, jealously, lust, hate, and selfishness had become woven into the fabric of mankind. But God would not let this sinful condition prevail. He loved the world so much that he sent his only Son to do what mankind could never do—to take upon himself, being sinless, all these sins and take them to the cross—to pay the penalty for our sins so that we could be forgiven. The penalty Jesus accepted was supremely severe because the sins were so severe. Didn't the words of Isaiah 700 years before prophesy these very events?

> *Surely he has borne our infirmities and carried our diseases; yet we accounted him stricken, struck down by God and afflicted.*
> *But he was wounded for our transgressions, crushed for our iniquities;*
> *Upon him was the punishment that made us whole, and by his bruises we are healed...the Lord has laid on him the iniquity of us all....*
> *By a perversion of justice he was taken away. Who could have imagined his future?*
> *For he was cut off from the land of the living, stricken for the transgression of my people....*
> *Through him the will of the Lord shall prosper. Out of his anguish he shall see light...*
> *the righteous one, my servant, shall make many righteous....*

And as we receive his sacrifice, his body and blood, we are accepted into God's family for all eternity. Jesus was indeed the Lamb of God who takes away the sin of the world as the Baptist had proclaimed. This was God's plan of redemption for mankind using no threat or force, but only love. No other way would have succeeded. The resurrection demonstrated Christ's victory over the Jewish religious authorities, the Roman Empire, death, and the power of Satan. It proclaimed the permanent promise of eternal life for all repentant believers.

John prayed silently, "How I thank you, Almighty God, for loving me so much. And how I love you Lord Jesus for taking away my sins, for cleansing my conscience, for bringing me out of death into life, and for making my search fruitful."

WHOOSH!!! Suddenly a mighty wind roared and swept through the house, shocking John out of his meditation. With it flashed a bright flame, which settled in the room, where they were seated. The flame separated and came to rest upon each of the disciples. John felt the power surge through his body and when he began to speak, the words came out in strange syllables like the language of another nation. The other disciples were affected in the same manner

The festival had filled Jerusalem with pilgrims from all over the Mediterranean world, and when they heard the sound like a tornado, they gathered together in the streets wondering what was taking place. The disciples, perceiving the commotion below, went out, each speaking in a different tongue. Parthians, Medes, people from Egypt, Libya, Rome, Arabia and other countries who were both Jews and proselytes heard the disciples speaking their own languages. Some, however, thought these men were drunk with new wine.

The word of this phenomenon quickly spread and soon the area around the house was packed with hundreds. Filled with the Holy Spirit, Peter, who had never before been an orator, spoke, "You Israelites listen to me. Jesus of Nazareth, a man known to you for deeds of power, wonders and signs that God did through him—this man was handed over to you according to God's preordained plan. You crucified and killed him by the hand of those outside the law. But God raised him up and freed him from death..."

Peter went on to explain, using the psalms of David, that this Jesus whom the Jews and Romans had crucified was both Lord and Messiah.

The people listening felt cut to the heart and said, "Brother, what must we do?"

Peter said, "Repent and be baptized in the name of Jesus Christ so you may be forgiven, and you will receive the gift of the Holy Spirit. For this promise is for you and your children and all that are far away, anyone that God calls to himself. Save yourselves from this corrupt generation." That day about 3000 were added to the company of believers.

John was astounded at Peter's ability to speak so effectively, but thankful and happy at the results. Filled with the Spirit from on high, the disciples did many deeds of power and wonder. As the days went quickly by, the community of followers grew. People started gathering in the larger homes. The services involved reading the Old Testament scripture including the prophets and psalms, listening to an interpretation of the word, and breaking of the bread and taking the wine, the body and blood of Jesus, interspersed with hymns of praise. The wealthy shared their possessions with the poor, and they all became known by the way they loved each other. They were even befriended and respected by the whole city.

John remembered the last commandment of the Lord about loving as he had loved. Somehow the love and devotion of the company of followers, even as they increased, was bringing that commandment to life. He was seeing the love of God (*agape*) manifested in human lives. The new fellowship was clearly the creation of Jesus. This love was closing even further the last gap in John's search for *ultimate meaning*. Experiencing the power of the Spirit had moved him closer as well.

One day Peter and John were going into the temple to pray when they came across a man crippled from birth. He was being laid at the Beautiful Gate so he could beg for alms. As the disciples passed by, he accosted them, asking for alms. Peter said, "Look at us. I have no silver or gold, but what I have I will give to you. In the name of Jesus Christ, stand up and walk!"

Peter took him by the hand and lifted him up. Immediately his ankles grew strong and he entered the temple with them, walking and leaping and praising God. The daunting plan of evangelizing the earth lay ahead, but with the power of the Spirit, the disciples were not overwhelmed.

XXV

Peter's Leadership

After the healing of the crippled man, the Jews in the temple gathered around Peter and John in amazement. In answer to their many questions, Peter spoke, "The God of Abraham, Isaac, and Jacob—the God of our ancestors has glorified his servant Jesus, whom you handed over to the Romans to be crucified. Pilate wanted to release him, but you chose a murderer to be released and instead killed the Author of Life, whom God raised from the dead. To this we are witnesses and it is by his name that this man has been healed. And now friends, we know that you and your rulers acted out of ignorance that the scriptures might be fulfilled.

"You must repent and turn to God for forgiveness—that your sins might be wiped out and that you may enjoy times of refreshment from the Lord. Moses himself said, 'God will raise up for you from your own people a prophet like me. You must listen to everything he tells you so that you might not be rooted out from the people.' You are descendants of the prophets and of the covenant God gave your ancestors, saying to Abraham that by his descendants all the families of the earth will be blessed. God sent his servant Jesus to you to bless you and turn you from your wicked ways."

While Peter and John were speaking, the temple police came and arrested them on instructions from the priests and the Sadducees, who were much annoyed that they were teaching in the name of Jesus. The next day along with the healed crippled man, they stood in the midst of the priests, rulers, elders and scribes who asked how they had healed the man.

Peter, who had become the voice of the followers of Jesus, said, "You question us about a good deed done to heal this man? Let it be known to you and to all the people of Israel that this man stands healed before you because of the name of Jesus Christ of Nazareth, whom you crucified and whom God raised from the dead." And he quoted the Psalm:

> *"The stone that was rejected by you, the builders;*
> *It has become the chief cornerstone."*

Peter continued, "There is salvation in no one else, for there is no other name under heaven by which we can be saved."

After dismissing the disciples, the council debated among themselves. They agreed that no one could discount the healing which had taken place, so they decided to warn the disciples to teach and heal no more in the name of Jesus. When Peter and John were brought back in and warned, Peter said, "Whether it is right to listen to you or to God, you must judge. But we cannot refrain from speaking what we have seen and heard."

After giving them a severe warning, they let them go. When they returned to their friends and reported all that the council had commanded them, the whole group lifted their voices in prayer. One of them said, "Sovereign Lord, who made the heaven, the earth, the sea and everything in it, you said through David by the Holy Spirit:

> *'Why did the Gentiles rage and the peoples imagine vain things? The kings of the earth took their stand, and the rulers have gathered together against the Lord and against his Messiah.'*

"For in this city the rulers gathered together against your holy servant Jesus to do what your plan had predestined. Now, Lord, look at their threats and grant to your servants to speak with boldness while you stretch forth your hand to heal, and signs and wonders are performed in the name of your servant Jesus."

Healing and signs continued to be performed in the name of Jesus and the disciples continued to be threatened and even flogged by the rulers. Peter in particular was healing the sick and doing the work of the Lord.

Organization and strategy were planned by the disciples in the upper room. As the number of converts continued to grow, the disciples appointed seven men of faith and good standing to help with the distribution of food and other matters. But persecution by the Sanhedrin continued, resulting in the stoning death of Stephen, one of the seven. The chief priests even appointed a special prosecutor named Paul to try and wipe out the new movement. Paul succeeded for a while, but became converted himself while on the road to Damascus to arrest the followers of Jesus, now called "the people of the Way."

Peter was called to Joppa where, by the name of Christ, he

raised a faithful young woman from the dead. Afterward, Peter went up on the roof to pray and had a vision. He saw a sheet being let down from heaven containing all kinds of four-footed creatures, reptiles and birds. A voice commanded him to eat. But Peter said, "Lord, I will never eat anything that is unclean or profane."

The voice answered, "Do not call profane anything the Lord has made." This continued three times.

About the same time, some messengers arrived from Caesarea from the house of Cornelius, a centurion of the Italian Cohort. Cornelius was a Gentile, a God fearing man who generously gave alms to the poor and prayed regularly to God. In a vision, Cornelius had been instructed to send messengers to Joppa to a man called Simon Peter—to ask him to come to Caesarea and instruct them concerning Jesus. When they confronted Peter with the request, he normally would have turned it down, being the house of a Gentile. But his vision persuaded him to go with them.

Arriving at the household of Cornelius, Peter was asked to speak God's message to them. After telling them the good news of Christ, the Spirit fell upon everyone in the house including the relatives and close friends of Cornelius, and they began to praise God and speak in tongues. Peter and the believers who had accompanied him were astounded that the Spirit had come upon the Gentiles. This experience altered Peter's heart toward Gentiles, and he called for water to baptize the entire household.

Up until this point, preaching the gospel had proceeded with relative peace, but persecution lay ahead for the disciples just as Jesus had predicted.

XXVI

Persecution

At this time King Herod began a violent persecution against the church. As James was walking to the temple, Herod's men seized him, carried him to Herod's palace, and put him in prison. Herod Agrippa had close connections with the chief priests and sided with them against the Way.

When John and many other members of the church found out about this aggressive act, they gathered together in front of Herod's palace to protest the arrest. They demanded that he send James out to them. Herod, in his own diabolical way, instructed his soldiers how to deliver James to the people of the Way.

Following the king's instructions, the soldiers opened the gate and formed a semicircle two soldiers deep with the wall at their backs. They lowered their spears to a horizontal position to form an impregnable line while two large guards brought James out, his hands tied behind his back. The guards forced James to a kneeling position.

John, suddenly realizing what was taking place, charged the soldiers with a loud cry, "NO!" The spears passed through his clothing and superficially pieced his flesh. At the same time one of the soldiers brought the flat side of his sword down upon John's head. The blow mercifully sent him into momentary oblivion.

One burly guard then grabbed James' hair and pulled his head forward, stretching his neck. The other raised a large, heavy sword and with one blow severed his head from his body. A cry of anguish went up from the people as the soldiers backed away and disappeared behind the walls, closing the gate.

Faithful friends picked up John and tied a sash tightly around his midsection to stop the bleeding. They then aroused him and carried him away to tend his wounds. Another group sent for a bier to take away James' body and lifeless head.

John recovered quickly from his wounds, but he, Salome, and Malachi could not be comforted. He could not accept the fact that his beloved older brother had been killed, and his mind wandered back over the many times James had mentored and defended him. He kept asking, "Lord, why did James have to die?" The only answer was not consoling. It lay in the mystery of what wicked men willfully do to the innocent. Only their faith and the companionship of Mary the mother of Jesus, sustained John, Salome, and Malachi through the funeral and the days following.

When Herod saw that this barbaric act had pleased the rulers of the Jews, he had Peter arrested and placed in prison to await the same fate as James. In order to fully secure him, Herod had him chained between two guards, with other guards on the prison door. That night the bright light of an angel appeared in the prison. The angel woke Peter and the chains fell from his legs and arms, and he motioned for the disciple to follow him. Peter still half asleep could not tell whether he was dreaming or not. They went through the door, which opened of its own accord, and right past the other guards. Peter soon found himself alone on the street as the angel disappeared.

The house of John Mark, a disciple of Jesus, was nearby, so Peter walked there. John Bar Zebedee and other disciples were in the house praying fervently for their leader. Peter knocked loudly at the outer gate. When the maid went to answer, she recognized Peter's voice, but was so shaken that she ran back into the house to tell the others. They answered, "It must be his spirit." But the maid insisted, and when they went to the gate and let Peter in, there were many loud cheers and praises to God. Peter and Rachel were hidden away by the church to prevent his being taken again.

In the morning Herod sent for Peter and was told he was not in the prison. He became so infuriated that he put the guards to death. Not long after this took place, Herod believing that he was a god, went out on the platform in the stadium at Caesarea to deliver a public address. The people, to curry his favor, kept shouting, "The voice of a god!" Suddenly Herod was seized with an excruciating pain and fell headlong off the platform and died. His ending was mourned by very few.

A measure of uncertain peace returned to Jerusalem. But it would not last for long because of the enmity, fear, and jealousy of the Jewish rulers.

XXVII

Acts Of The Church

During the next few years the church began to take the gospel outside of Jerusalem. Philip, one of the seven, carried the gospel to the city of Samaria. John and Peter followed Philip there and prayed for the people of that city who experienced the Holy Spirit. John recalled his first trip into the country of Samaria when he wanted to call down fire from heaven upon a village which rejected the Lord. He was admonished by Jesus, who pointed out that he came to save not to judge mankind.

Philip had also preached the gospel to an Ethiopian, who was returning to his country. This man, a court official of the queen, believed and was baptized by Philip in a pool of water beside the road. He carried the gospel back to his country.

Some of Jesus' followers, who had left Jerusalem during the persecution resulting in Stephen's death, settled in Antioch of Syria and preached the gospel there. Many Greeks had accepted their preaching and a church was established consisting of Jews and Gentiles. It was in this church that the people of The Way were first called Christians.

John's heart had changed so much as he had continued his fellowship with Jesus. He had finally learned that love was just as powerful and important as truth. This introspection was made even clearer to him as he found most people in Samaria responding to the love of God as revealed in the gospel. When John and Peter weren't traveling, there was more than all the disciples could handle in caring for and ministering to the people of Jerusalem and Judea. The fortune of Malachi and what was left of the inheritances of James and John were devoted to the ministry as were the resources of other wealthy Christians. Many times John put in long days and worked into the night until completely exhausted.

He did find time now and then to call on Deborah, but he had to be careful. The high priest had seen John brought before the Sanhedrin, so John had to avoid him. The servants realized that the former fisherman had been with Jesus, but if anything they were sympathetic and some had committed to the Lord including Deborah. Their meetings took place mostly at night as they took long walks around the city, telling each other about their childhood experiences and laughing together. John found that he needed the love and companionship of Deborah. Their "goodnights" were always very tender as they embraced and kissed.

John was very tempted to ask Deborah to marry him, but each time it came to mind, he thought about Peter and Rachel. That couple very seldom saw each other, and the relationship was strained. The Lord's work would always take precedence with both Peter and John, and to maintain a household at the same time was a difficult matter. The sexual attraction between John and Deborah was very present, but their Jewish upbringing and commitment to the Lord's teaching was stronger, so they resisted and remained celibate.

John's other free nights were spent in the company of the mother of Jesus and Salome. The two women, having known each other in their childhood days in Nazareth, had grown very close. It was fortunate that Mary had been there when James was killed and had helped Salome through that difficult period. The three of them talked long into the night about Jesus, his childhood, and the early signs of his identity.

The years began to go by swiftly as the apostles worked hard to carry the word and love of Jesus into all parts of Judea and the adjoining countryside while desperately trying to avoid the Jewish rulers and their constant opposition. In the meanwhile, Paul, the converted prosecutor, had joined the church at Antioch. That congregation consisting of Jews, Greeks, blacks and whites, rich and poor had been especially filled with the Holy Spirit, who set aside Paul and Barnabas to carry the word of God into the world. Barnabas was among the first Christians in Jerusalem and was loved and respected by the entire church. Paul had become one of the most gifted and charismatic preachers in the church and was a man of enormous energy and determination. Their remarkable missionary journey establishing churches in Cyprus and Asia Minor was a miraculous accomplishment, the news of which traveled quickly to Jerusalem and to the apostles.

The question of Gentile churches was dealt with successfully at the Jerusalem Council of the church, when it was decided that Gentiles were fully acceptable if they would refrain from sexual immorality, from eating the blood of animals slaughtered for food, and from all things polluted by idols. This decision was greatly encouraging to the Christians of Antioch and the new churches, and the spiritual dynamo of Antioch continued to send forth missionaries.

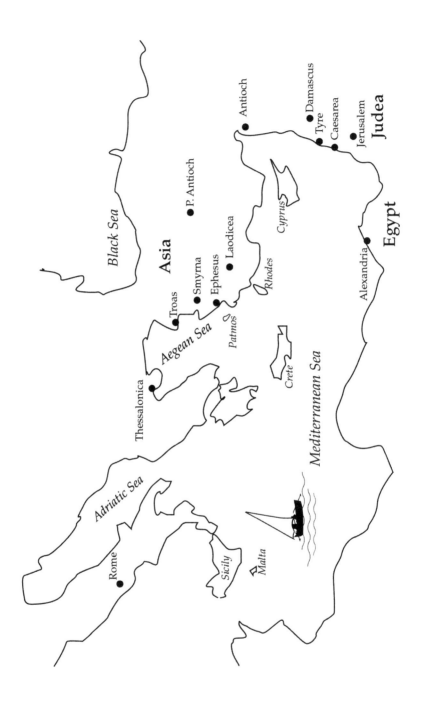

Peter and John both realized that the time had come for the apostles to go forth into the world. They called the apostles together in the upper room and began with a long period of prayer and an appeal for the Spirit to assist them. Then the discussion began. Some of them were married and questioned whether they could leave the city for long periods; others were not as young and strong as they used to be and thereby wondered about their fitness. There was a legitimate concern also for the church in Judea, about it being deprived of its most dedicated and experienced leadership. Peter and John, perhaps understanding the instruction of the Lord more than the others, held out for a world wide mission. They both believed that the Spirit would compensate for and take care of their weaknesses.

Finally, it was decided that most of the apostles would be assigned different areas of the Mediterranean world. The oldest and some who were married with families would stay in Jerusalem and continue leading the mother church as well as supporting the surrounding area. Peter would be sent to Rome, while John would go to Asia, probably Ephesus. Others were assigned North Africa, such as Alexandria in Egypt and some even to Spain. The time was 58 AD, twenty five years after the resurrection.

John dreaded the thought of telling Deborah about this decision, and he wondered what unusual experiences awaited him in faraway Asia.

XXVIII

To The Ends Of The Earth

Many duties had to be taken care of before the departure of the apostles. All nearby congregations had to be visited and informed, personal properties and affairs had to be sold or dealt with, advance reservations on ships made etc. All these took several weeks to complete. In the meanwhile, the apostles met as frequently as possible to pray for the missions and the churches left behind.

One event of immense importance shook the entire church. Mary, the beloved mother of Jesus passed away in her sleep. Christians knew that she longed to be with her Son, but her departure took away the person closest to the Lord. It was also a reminder that the apostles' time on earth was limited, and the commission of Jesus needed to be pursued deliberately. Almost every Christian in the entire province of Judea attended the funeral, which was held in the garden where Jesus and the disciples used to meet. Messengers were also sent to far away churches which held memorial services for Mary.

John, the disciple closest to Mary, felt the greatest loss, since the Lord had appointed him to be her son. There was also that spiritual quality about Mary which reminded him so much of Jesus and was such a comfort to be around.

When Deborah heard that the apostles were planning to leave Jerusalem, she felt a sharp stab in her heart. She had long since realized that they probably would never be married, but just being with John gave her a peaceful sense of fulfillment. John put off their farewell meeting as long as possible. He also felt the intense pain of leaving her, and knew that he would never love another woman. The thought of not seeing her again brought tears to his eyes and left a lump in his throat. Their last night together brought pledges of eternal love between fond kisses and embraces.

The last meeting of the apostles in the upper room was also a time of intense emotion. John's best friend Peter was headed far away to Rome, which meant they might never lay eyes on each other again. There was a similar sense of sadness in the hearts of all of them. On the other hand, each could feel the tug of the Holy Spirit to move ahead with the commission of Jesus.

John felt much better about his mother when some of the remaining apostles moved into the Malachi house with Salome. He knew that she would have the best and most loyal protection available, and that they would protect her with their lives.

After bidding Salome goodbye, John traveled to Caesarea to catch a ship bound for Ephesus and Corinth. The voyage was pleasant with no bad weather, and the ship passed Rhodes and docked temporarily at Ephesus where John disembarked. The great missionary Paul had just left Ephesus a few weeks earlier, and John found the church prospering even in a pagan city devoted to the goddess Artemis. The Christian leaders Aquila and Priscilla, who had done so much to enhance Paul's ministry, were still living in Ephesus and they, upon hearing of John's arrival, immediately invited him into their home. The Christians in Ephesus were delighted and honored to have one of the original disciples moving there.

On the first day of the week at the regular gathering, John was introduced and related to the congregation all the news from Jerusalem including Mary's death. He then preached a sermon about the mission of the church.

Over the first weeks of his stay in Ephesus, John learned much about this important city. Ephesus was a large Roman city in Asia with a population of over 200,000. It was a center of trade and commerce, being a seaport situated on a river close to the Mediterranean. It also supported Greek culture and boasted a theater seating 25,000 people. The temple to Artemis was at this time one of the wonders of the world, being much larger and more ornate than the Parthenon in Athens. Pagan religion occasionally clashed with Christianity, but on the whole there was a fairly peaceful coexistence. The Roman officials frowned on any type of civil unrest and helped to keep order.

Six prominent cities surrounded Ephesus; they were in easy traveling distance with their citizens making regular trips to Ephesus for cultural, religious and commercial reasons. Each one of these cities had the fledgling beginning of a Christian church due to the influence of Paul. They needed leadership and support, and John fell right in with this missionary need. He began visiting them on a regular schedule, preaching, baptizing, and providing the direct link with Jesus so much needed. He also appointed elders to oversee each church.

One day John visited Smyrna. He was preaching the gospel

when he noticed a young man in the congregation whose handsome visage and rapt attention clearly stood out. After the service John met the youth and was impressed by his intelligence and interest in the faith. Later John told the chief elder about the young man. "He is a fine looking lad and more importantly, shows an unusual interest in the gospel." John asked the elder, "Would you take him into your confidence and guidance? He has the qualities and talents to become a future leader of the church."

The elder consented to the challenge and in the days and weeks that followed he worked diligently with the young man, teaching him the stories and parables of Jesus and imparting to him the theology of the church. He took a personal interest in him, inviting him into his home for meals and even becoming like a father to him.

For a while the young man responded positively and seemed to avidly enjoy the instruction and faith. But as he grew older, he began keeping company with other youths his own age. He fell in with some who were undisciplined, rowdy, and wild, taking on their ways. Before long he joined a gang of young robbers and with his superior strength and intelligence soon became their leader.

Several months went by and time came again for John to visit Smyrna. John remembered the young man and asked the elder how his young understudy was doing. The elder sheepishly had to confess what had happened. John was shocked; he asked for a horse and directions to the bandit's lair. Riding right into the campsite, he was stopped by the guards who wanted to dispose of him. However, he asked to see their leader, but when the young man saw John, he became so ashamed that he turned and ran the other way. Even though the youth was twenty years younger than John, the apostle would not give up the chase. Finally John shouted, "Why do you run from me, son? I am old enough to be your father, and I will account to Christ for you. I will pay back anything that you owe—I will even give my life for you if necessary as Christ gave his life for us all. Please stop! Christ sent me after you."

At this the young man stopped and threw down his weapons. He lowered his head and began to weep bitterly. John caught up, threw his arms around him, and declared again that he had found pardon for him in Christ. John brought him back to the church, interceded for him with much prayer, and fasted with him to bring him back under the control of Christ. John made amends for all that the young man had done and did not leave until he was fully restored. Changed by John's witness and concern for him, the young man, Jason, became a faithful church worker. By such a heroic effort and dozens of others, John built up the church in Asia.

After a few years, the cities of Smyrna, Pergamum, Thyatira, Sardis, Philadelphia and Laodicea boasted active congregations similar to Ephesus. John appointed a bishop over these cities and then began to travel even greater distances for the gospel. He went as far as Pisidian Antioch to the east, Troas to the north. and Rhodes to the south. He worked very intensely and the years passed swiftly, but every so often thoughts of Salome, Deborah, the apostles in Jerusalem, Peter and the others would come to mind.

John would get lost in thought wondering how they all were doing. Distance prevented him from getting the latest news from Jerusalem. Finally a Christian from Jerusalem showed up. He told John how the Zealots had taken over the city, and that a large scale battle was in progress. The Romans under Vespasian and Titus had marched against Israel with a large army, and Jerusalem had been under siege for some time.

But his other news was just as devastating to John. Peter, his life long friend, had been crucified in Rome by the order of

Nero. It had occurred in the arena during the games for the amusement of the emperor and the crowd. The report was that the big fisherman had defied the emperor by insisting that he be crucified upside down; he had shouted that he was not worthy to be crucified like his Lord. The report shocked John as had the beheading of James, and he had to excuse himself and go to his room to hide his sobs and keen feeling of bereavement. The charismatic missionary Paul also had been executed during Nero's persecution, the emperor having falsely blamed Christians for the fire which destroyed much of Rome.

John found it hard to believe that his big, muscular friend was gone. He could see him now stripped to the waist, hauling in the net and doing the work of three ordinary men. He also pictured him at his finest hour, addressing the crowds in the streets of Jerusalem or the rulers of the Sanhedrin. He knew Peter's work in Europe and Rome must have been very effective. Boyhood memories also flashed before his eyes—Peter always defending John or teaching him the finer points of fishing and life. He remembered how Jesus had handled his pardoning of Peter at the seashore and how Jesus appointed him to head the apostles. With sadness he recalled the prophecy of Jesus concerning how Peter would glorify God in his crucifixion. And he wondered how many of the twelve were still alive.

With so many loved ones and friends in danger, John determined to leave Ephesus for a while and return to Jerusalem. It took several days to find passage on a southern bound ship and several more days to reach Caesarea. More than three weeks elapsed before he finally came within sight of the city. It was a sight he would never forget.

XXIX

Jerusalem Destroyed

When still far off, John could see the pillar of smoke pouring from the city. As he drew closer he could not believe his eyes. The great walls were a mass of crumbled ruins. Where the beloved temple had stood gleaming in the sunlight, there was nothing but rubble. In fact, it appeared as if a great fire and earthquake had swept the city, leaving almost every structure either burned or partially destroyed. The hills for miles around were void of all trees, leaving hundreds of stumps. The Romans had used the wood to build siege towers, catapults and many battering rams. But perhaps the worst part was the stench, which penetrated the air for miles. Piles of rotting corpses could be seen in every direction. The city had been utterly destroyed and the people with it. The year was 70 AD.

John tried to keep his mind from imagining what might have happened to the Jerusalem apostles. Even worse, he was deeply shaken when he thought of his mother and Deborah. He knew how ruthless and barbaric soldiers could be when a city was sacked after a long and bloody siege. He tried to put off terrifying thoughts about their capture to be taken to Rome for the arena or even more chilling—the possibility that they already had been raped and murdered.

Since a small garrison of Roman soldiers had been left there, John had to move furtively, hiding behind burned out walls and even piles of corpses. Tying a cloth over his nose, he slowly made his way to the Malachi house. It too lay half burned out with only some walls standing. He encountered several bodies, going from one to another and dreading what he might find; however, he failed to recognize any of them. He continued to search in the outside court for the bodies of his mother, Malachi, and the other disciples, but they were nowhere to be found. He knew he could not get close to the palace of the high priest, where Deborah had worked and lived, since that area was where the remaining Roman soldiers appeared to be bivouacked. Moving slowly to avoid small detachments of soldiers, he made his way out of the city.

Not knowing what else to do, he headed for Capernaum. He had brought with him two loaves of bread, which sustained him on the way. He slept out under the stars and again the memory of many happy days on this road came over him, but the nightmare of Salome and Deborah's fate consumed him. As he moved farther from Jerusalem, the countryside began to look more normal, and he soon found himself traveling beside his beloved Sea of Galilee. There were more small bands of Roman soldiers to avoid, so he had to be careful. The villages along the sea were not harmed, allowing him to purchase some salt-fish, which brought back pleasant memories.

As he walked along, Jesus' astonishing prophecy came back to him: "...the days are coming when your enemies will set up ramparts around your walls and close you in on every side. They will crush you and your children to the ground and not one stone will be left here upon another. All will be thrown down because you did not recognize the time of God's visitation." And in the same discourse, "then those who are in Judea must flee to the mountains, the one in the field must not turn back to get a coat." John then knew that the Master had prophesied the destruction of Jerusalem followed by a description of end times.

Early one morning as he was preparing to start his journey again, he came face to face with a young Roman soldier, who had left his unit to bathe in the sea. A sudden rage flew over John as the slaughter of his people flashed through his mind. He charged the Roman at full speed, driving him to the ground. At the same time John pulled a dagger from the soldier's side and raised it with deadly intent. But strangely, he could not drive it home. The Spirit stayed his hand. Tossing the dagger into the bushes, John arose and left the dazed Roman on the ground.

Coming into Capernaum, he went directly to his old family home, which looked very much the same as when he had left all those years ago. He entered the gate and walked into the kitchen, not knowing really what to expect. At first he thought he might be dreaming, for there with her back turned to him was his mother Salome. Her hair had turned silver, but he would have recognized her anywhere. "Mother", he quietly called, and she turned around and with a gasp of surprise and tears she embraced her son.

"Jerusalem and our magnificent temple have been destroyed," he added, "how did you escape?"

"After the Zealots took over, we all knew the Romans would not stand for it. Christians were warned to leave the city; we felt we were following the instructions of the Lord. The apostles and their families left early, and we escaped at the last moment before the Romans closed the siege."

Puzzled at the use of *we,* John asked, "Who went with you?"

"Oh, John, I have some glorious news. Two days before I departed, Deborah, whose family had already pulled out, left the high priest's palace and came to our home. She was afraid to stay there any longer and also believed that I would need an escort out of the city. I probably wouldn't have made it without her."

John's heart skipped a beat. Was it possible? "Where is she now?"

"She went to a neighbor's house to borrow some milk. She should be back by now."

At that moment, Deborah opened the kitchen door. She almost dropped the pitcher when she saw John. "John is it really you?" She set the pitcher down and embraced the apostle, not wanting to let him go. "How did you know? How did you get here?"

The three sat down at the table and related their miraculous and exciting stories. John then asked, "Tell me about Malachi?"

"He was spared most of this conflict. He passed away three years ago," Salome replied. John's thoughts drifted back to Malachi's influence on his life, and he said a silent prayer for his generous and affable uncle.

Finally, John said, "I guess the family renting this house left in fear of the Romans. I'm also not sure we are safe even in Galilee. The slaughter in Jerusalem was horrendous. It was as if the Romans wanted to completely wipe out the Jewish race."

Salome asked, "What can we do?"

"We must try to find our way to Ephesus. I have many friends there even among the officials, and I must get back to my work." Getting out of Israel would definitely be a problem, John thought. The Romans would be all over Caesarea so they would have to find another port. Traveling over land with the two women could be dangerous.

"The closest good port might be Tyre in Syria, where a good Christian community flourishes."

That night after supper John looked at the old maps showing the roads north toward Tyre. The road through Gischala looked promising and was probably a three or four day's journey by foot. Early the next morning after packing a lunch of bread, salt-fish, and dried dates, the three joined other refugees fleeing Israel. They slept on the ground wrapped in their cloaks under myriads of stars, but felt safe as they were surrounded by dozens of fleeing Jews. Pushing it as fast as the women could, they made it to Tyre the afternoon of the third day. Roman soldiers were rarely seen because they had been called to fight in the war against Israel. The Christians found lodging with others of the faith who were glad and pleased to have an apostle with them. Three days later with the help of some gold coins Salome had saved from Zebedee's estate, they boarded a merchant ship bound for Ephesus.

Commercial ships often took on passengers, but provided no rooms or facilities. When the weather was good, the passengers slept on deck. During rough weather or rainy days, they had to stay in the hold with the cargo. On this journey, the weather was generally fair even though the fall season was approaching. In fact the voyage provided a pleasant respite from the fury and slaughter back in Israel. With all the recent traumas, John dreamed of a peaceful and profitable time in Asia, doing evangelistic work while having the two women he loved most at his side.

As for the destruction of the temple, as much as he had admired and loved it, he remembered the Lord's words to the Samaritan woman at the well, "Woman, believe me the time is coming when you will worship the Father neither on this mountain nor in Jerusalem. But the hour is coming and in fact is already here when true worshipers will worship the Father in spirit and truth, for the Father is seeking such to worship him. God is spirit, and those who worship him must worship in spirit and truth."

XXX

A Difficult Decision

John's arrival in Ephesus was marked with celebrations and special church services. The entire city welcomed him, even pagan worshipers of Artemis and Roman officials who highly respected him. Salome and Deborah were accepted and welcomed as well, and the church bought a nice home for the apostle, soon to be one of the last of the twelve. John reveled in the good will and love shown to him, Salome and Deborah, but he was anxious to get back to work visiting and assisting the churches of Asia.

Although Vespasian (and his son Titus) had been responsible for the horrible massacre and destruction of Jerusalem, the office of emperor to which he had been called, seemed to broaden his character. The following decade of his rule proved to be one of the most peaceful and stable of recent emperors, and the Christian church, so used to persecution, continued to flourish and expand.

When John was not traveling to the churches of Asia, he was enjoying life with his mother Salome and his other love, Deborah. John was now 65 years old and Deborah,59. The years had kept them mostly apart, but their love never diminished. He wondered again about asking her to marry him and even discussed the subject with Salome. She generally approved but indicated it was John's decision. To John, Deborah was just as attractive as when they first met. She had that deep beauty of character as well as a lovely appearance, and John had held his age well. His short black beard showed some flecks of white, and his hairline had slightly receded showing a small bald spot on the back. He still had the handsome quality of the Zebedee men.

Late one afternoon as the sun was low in the sky, John asked Deborah to go for a walk. They found a bench in one of the city's small parks and as the sun was setting, he said, "Deborah, now that I've found you again, I want to marry you."

She didn't reply at first, but finally with tears in her eyes she spoke softly to him. "John, you know how I have always loved you and I always will. I am too old to bear you any children, and I do very truly and honestly know and respect your first love and even possibly mine—our Lord and Savior. You are called to the highest duty and quest possible and its revelation to all people. I could not bear to distract you even a little bit from that high calling. No. I am content to be near you and share your faith. Having said that, she leaned over and kissed him gently on the cheek.

They walked home in silence, holding hands. John was crestfallen at first, but later as he prayed about it and thought it over thoroughly, he realized Deborah was right. In addition to his duties as the apostle to Asia, he felt the Lord was calling him to some further undertaking, and it would require all that he could give it.

XXXI

Searching For The Call

John's area of responsibility now included much of what was then called Asia, extending from Ephesus on the west to Galatia and Pamphylia on the east and from north of Troas to Rhodes on the south. It was a large geographical area with a growing Christian population and a need for more bishops. Just making the rounds of the churches took almost a year and being the only apostle in that area, he was very much in demand. The time he could spend with Salome and Deborah was getting shorter each year, and with Salome in her mid eighties he knew that her time on earth was limited.

John was constantly praying for the Lord to make clear to him what his new calling was. He knew it would eventually be revealed to him, and it came one day when he was in Ephesus between church visitations. A group of elders from the church in Ephesus came to his home with a very special request. They asked John to write his account of the three year ministry of

Jesus—to write another gospel. In their association with John they had felt the closeness between John and the Lord. There were already three gospels written and being circulated in the churches, and John wondered whether another was needed. He promised the group he would give it serious consideration and much prayer.

After the delegation left, he broached the subject with Salome and Deborah. They both agreed that John's special relationship with the Lord was sufficient reason for undertaking the task. He prayed that night, "Oh, Lord, this would be an awesome responsibility. I am willing, but I ask you for some kind of confirmation."

Two days later a group from Smyrna, completely independent of the first group and led by his former convert, Jason, came to his house. When they made the same request of John, he felt like he had his confirmation. He would have to make time available to give it his very best effort. He also knew that the Spirit would have to lead him, so he prayed each day for this special presence to make his mission successful. He found that writing late at night, after the women retired, to be most fruitful. He could continue writing this way even when he was off on a church visitation. Each writing session was preceded by earnest prayer for the Spirit's guidance.

He began his gospel with John the Baptist's call for repentance and preparation for the Messiah. John's time with the Baptist and his early introduction to Jesus gave him a clear prospective of the beginning of Jesus' ministry. Some nights would be productive and others would simply be filled with prayerful thought. John continued working on the gospel in this manner—not at all rushed, but thoughtfully and prayerfully.

A year went by and found John with a fairly complete outline. During the next year he would think and pray again about each event or discourse and at times add more flesh to the bones. He found Deborah and Salome to be good editors, correcting his grammar and questioning some of his sentence construction. When he returned from a church visitation, he would submit his writings to the two women for corrections. But always the facts were entirely his and those of the Holy Spirit. Two years of this tireless effort produced a complete manuscript, but John knew something was missing. Then late one night as he diligently sought the guidance of the Spirit, it came to him. The gospel did not begin with the Baptist's call; it began with the Father, who sent his Son into the world to save mankind. But try as he may, he could not summon the words and message for the beginning of his gospel. John believed, however, that in time it would be revealed to him. This revelation would complete his own search for the Infinite. He needed to put the manuscript away and wait for the Spirit's instruction.

It was during this time that Salome at 89 passed away. She had always been a great supporter and source of strength for John. Her love had borne him through some of the hard times, and he deeply loved her. He knew, however, that her faith was strong, and that she had gone to be with the Lord. And even though his family consisted of all the converts he had brought into the faith as well as those Paul had converted, only Deborah was left in his own household.

John's hard work with the churches, which gave him a feeling of fulfillment, made the years go by swiftly. A decade passed, Vespasian died, giving the empire to Titus, his son, who was also backed by the army. Titus died from an illness after a short reign from 79 to 81 AD. But then storm clouds formed again for the church when Vespasian's other son Domitian, became emperor. The first part of his reign was positive, but he became obsessed with emperor worship. He first deified his father Vespasian, and then his brother Titus. He even built temples to honor them.

It naturally followed that he proclaimed himself a god to be worshiped by the people of the empire. All who would not worship him and make sacrifices to him including Christians were persecuted. His dictatorial rule made him many enemies in the Roman senate, and some senators were stripped of their property, banished, or killed.

Emperor worship had been a real issue for Christians earlier, and now it assumed an even grimmer nature. There was no way Christians could conform to this *religion,* and as Domitian grew more dictatorial and tyrannical, he began to crack down not only in Rome, but in the faraway provinces. He issued a decree that if Christian or other leaders did not conform to emperor worship and make sacrifices to him, they were to be put to death.

The Roman governor of Asia was headquartered in Ephesus, the largest and most prominent city in that province. He and his whole staff had come to know John as honorable, kind, and a friend to all the citizens of Ephesus. John had spent many hours praying for the sick and assisting the poor. In order not to put him to death, they exiled him to the island of Patmos where he would become a prisoner in the Roman penal colony and forced to work in the rock quarry.

John was given three days to settle his affairs and spend time with Deborah. He was now 87 years old. His hair and beard had turned white, and his body thin. He was not feeble, however, a credit to his early days as a fisherman and his dedication to the Lord. He bade an emotional farewell to Deborah and embraced her before leaving. He then went to the port and boarded a ship with numerous other prisoners. His gospel was still not complete, and he would not circulate it until the Spirit spoke to him.

XXXII
Patmos Penal Colony

Patmos was a small crescent shaped island, six miles wide and only ten miles long. It had been formed in prehistoric times by the eruption of a volcano and consequently its landscape was rocky and barren. Near its midpoint was a natural harbor, which served as a haven for merchant ships bound on long journeys. Its coast line was mostly rugged and rocky with only one or two beaches. It had proven to be useful to Roman emperors as a place to banish criminals and political enemies.

The journey from Ephesus was a short one, and when the ship arrived in the harbor, the prisoners were hustled off to be registered. They were then marched off to a compound, where they would live out their sentences with only the protection of open sheds and mats made from any type of vegetation they could gather.

Early the next morning John was shackled to two other prisoners and taken to the quarry, which had opened up one side of a hill. He would spend the entire day there struggling with the rock. The prisoners worked in groups of three. One worked with a quarry hammer, which was a heavy wedge shaped metal head pressed onto a round wooden shaft. The second prisoner was given a sharper metal wedge and the other a larger hammer. The quarry hammer was used to open a line in the rock taking advantage of natural cleavages. The metal wedge was then inserted into that shallow trench and pounded with the heavier hammer. The wedge-man and hammer-man occasionally traded places.

As the rocks piled up, they were rolled or lifted onto low carts by other prisoners and pulled to the harbor by oxen. The work was back breaking and lasted all day in the hot sun. Roman guards with short whips assured that very little rest was allowed. Water was brought in, more to keep the prisoners going than to provide any relief or comfort.

If a prisoner fainted from the heat, he was simply dragged along by the other two until he finally revived or even died. The prisoners were fed one meal a day after the work was done, and that meal was a thin, unappetizing gruel with one piece of sometimes stale or moldy bread. John soon realized that only the fittest survived such treatment, and that the purpose of the entire undertaking was more punishment than production. Even so, he sometimes shared his meal with those who were weak and shaky. The shackles were never removed with the exception of once a month when the prisoners were marched to the sea and allowed to bath themselves in the salt water.

In spite of these conditions John soon converted the other two members of his group. Others who heard only snatches of his conversation together with psalms and hymns of praise longed to hear more, and the guard who was over his section became interested as well. At his advanced age, he did grow weaker, but his continued stamina under brutal and harsh conditions amazed everyone. Many mornings he would arise singing the words of Isaiah:

" ...those who wait upon the Lord shall renew
their strength, they shall mount up with wings like
eagles, they shall run and not be weary,
they shall walk and not faint."

The repetition of these words together with his amazing resilient energy earned him the appellation of "the Eagle." That name would stick with him the rest of his life and would come to signify his distinction as an evangelist.

Weeks and months passed by causing John to lose all sense of time. It was as if this dreadful incarceration was to become his home forever.

Arrius, the Roman tribune in charge of the colony, had come from an aristocratic family. His two older brothers had entered the political field, one becoming a senator. Arrius had chosen the army and his bravery and loyalty had distinguished him at an early age, enabling him to obtain the rank of tribune. Domitian, after becoming emperor, became an avowed enemy of the aristocracy and most of the senators, and he diminished their families in any way that he could. He confiscated the property of Arrius' brother, the senator, and he appointed Arrius to head the prison colony at Patmos, an assignment considered to be a dead end.

It was almost as if Arrius himself had been banished to the barren island. The drudgery of dealing month after month with real and political prisoners was not at all edifying, and there were no social affairs, theater, or arena entertainment to provide a respite or relief from the dullness of the penal colony. After three years of this miserable assignment, Arrius had become ill tempered and depressed and often took out his feelings on the prisoners. At the first sign of any problem he would order that the ration be reduced or the work hours extended. It seemed as if in some diabolical way he enjoyed punishing the prisoners and seeing them suffer. These harsh measures always resulted in more sickness and death and instilled an intense hatred for the tribune among the prisoners.

After John had spent almost a year in these desperate circumstances, one night a guard woke him up, unshackled his chains and led him to the quarters of the tribune. Arrius had developed a very high fever, which unabated for three days, threatened his life. The guard, knowing about John's faith and acts of kindness, asked John to pray for the Roman. It wasn't easy to pray for a man whose orders had produced such suffering in the colony. John even hesitated at first to comply until the words of Jesus enveloped his heart. *"But I say to you love your enemies and pray for those who persecute you."*

Perhaps this occasion was closing the gap one notch tighter in John's search. He knelt before the bed of the tribune and prayed, "Oh God, this man has caused only hardship and death for the poor men in his charge, but your Son, Jesus has taught us to pray for those who maliciously use us and cause us much pain and suffering. Therefore, Father, I earnestly pray in the name of Jesus for the fever to leave this man. I ask that he might be restored to perfect health and that his heart be changed as well."

The next day went as usual with no word concerning the tribune. But the following night the same guard woke John again and this time led him out of the compound to the other side of the island. John wondered what his fate was going to be, but he followed the guard. After a long walk they climbed a hill and half way down the other side came upon a cave. The guard simply said to John. "This is your new lodging. Food and water will be brought to you each day along with any other necessities. You have the gratitude of the tribune, whose fever left shortly after you prayed for him. Stay away from the compound and the quarry and try not to be seen." With that the guard turned and left an astonished apostle. That night John slept well on a real mat and thanked God for this sudden turn of events.

XXXIII

Freedom And Apocalypse

The bright sun shining through the entrance of the cave woke John up. From the cave mouth he could see the blue water of the Aegean Sea. His new freedom and good fortune still seemed like a dream. Fruit and fresh bread had already been left at the entrance. After savoring his first breakfast in more than a year, John left the cave and carefully began to explore the island. Freedom from the ever present chains made him jump and leap and praise God as the healed cripple had done so many years ago.

He climbed the hill to get a more impressive view of his location. From there he could see a much higher point less than a half mile away so he hiked toward it, still being careful not to be seen. When he reached the high point, the view was spectacular. He could see much of the island and the port where he had arrived. Moreover, he could see miles out to sea with two other islands visible because of their high peaks. He found a ledge where he could sit, so this spot became a favorite place which he visited often. The natural beauty of the island, the sea and sky was breathtaking.

One day as he sat on the summit overlooking the sea, a short rain storm blew in with its usual thunder and lightning. The rain obscured the other islands and afterward the sea became calm and a rainbow almost encircled the island. John beheld such magnificent views with great wonder and praise for the Creator.

His now familiar guard, whom he had converted, brought him his supper one afternoon. His name was Gaius and he occasionally would have a short conversation with John.

"Sir, I think you would like to know that the tribune has increased the daily prisoner meals to two and has substantially improved their quality. He has also ordered a rest period during the middle of the day with ample water being brought in and care for the sick. The prisoners find it hard to believe, but they are very grateful."

John with a smile of appreciation said a silent prayer of thanksgiving to the Lord. Before Gaius left, John requested some writing materials.

One Lord's Day, Sunday, John left the cave for a morning walk. Suddenly the Spirit came upon him and he heard a loud voice like a trumpet saying, "Write in a book what you see and hear and send it to the seven churches, to Ephesus and to Smyrna and to Pergamum, to Thyatira, to Sardis, to Philadelphia and to Laodicea." (These were the seven churches where Paul and John had preached the word of Christ in the beginning of the mission to Asia.) The ensuing visions were spectacular, awesome, and terrifying, and took John through many vivid scenes leading to end times.

When the visions disappeared, John found himself alone where he had stood when the Spirit came upon him. Gathering his senses, he rushed back to the cave, took out the writing supplies and began to record the visions. He had witnessed so much he simply could not recall it all, but he wrote:

I turned and saw seven golden lamp stands and in

their midst one like the Son of Man. He was clothed with a long robe and with a golden sash across his chest. His hair was white as snow, his eyes burned like a flame, and his feet were like burnished bronze. In his hand he held seven stars and from his mouth came a sharp two edged sword and his face shown like the shining sun. When he spoke his voice was like the sound of many waters.

When I beheld him, I fell at his feet as though dead. But the Man placed his hand on my shoulder and said, "Do not be afraid; I am the first and the last. I was dead and see I am now alive forever, and I have the keys of Death and of Hades. Now write what you have seen, what is, and what will take place after this. As for the stars, they are the angels of the seven churches, and the lamp stands are the seven churches. The Son of Man then dictated letters to the seven churches, outlining their strengths and weaknesses and what they should do.

In the next vision, I was in an unfamiliar place. I heard the same voice like a trumpet saying, "Come up here and I will show you what must take place after this." Seeing an open door, I peered in. To my amazement I was looking at the throne room of heaven. The One seated there on the throne shone like precious stones and a rainbow which looked like an emerald encircled him. Around the throne stood twenty four other thrones and seated on the thrones were twenty four elders dressed in white with golden crowns upon their heads. From the throne there came rumblings of thunder and lightning. In front of the throne I saw something like a sea of glass, like crystal.

The vision went on further describing the heavenly

163

throne room and four living creatures on the sides of the throne. And when the four living creatures gave glory and honor and thanks to the One on the throne, the twenty four elders fell before the One seated on the throne, and worshiped the One who lives forever and ever; they cast their crowns before the throne and sang,

> *"You are worthy, our Lord and God,*
> *to receive glory and honor and power,*
> *for you created all things,*
> *and by your will they existed*
> *and were created."*

Then I saw in the right hand of the One seated on the throne a scroll written on the inside and on the back and sealed with seven seals; and I saw a mighty angel proclaiming with a loud voice, "Who is worthy to open the scroll and break its seals?" And no one in heaven or earth was able to open the scroll (which would show what was to come). And I began to weep bitterly because no one was found worthy to open the scroll.

Then one of the elders said to me, "Do not weep. See the Lion of the tribe of Judah, the Root of David has conquered so that he can open the scroll and its seven seals." Then I saw a Lamb as if it had been slaughtered, having seven horns and seven eyes, which are the seven spirits of God sent out into all the earth. He (the Lamb) went and took the scroll from the One seated on the throne. When he had taken the scroll, the four living creatures and the twenty four elders fell before the Lamb, each holding a harp and a golden bowl full of incense, which are the prayers of the saints. They sang a new song,

> *"You are worthy to take the*
> *scroll and to open its seals,*
> *For you were slaughtered and by*
> *your blood you ransomed for God*
> *saints from every tribe and language*
> *and people and nation;*
> *You have made them to be a kingdom*
> *and priests serving our God,*
> *and they will reign on earth."*

Then I looked and heard the voice of myriads of myriads and thousands of thousands of angels singing with the four living creatures and the elders,

> *"Worthy is the Lamb that was*
> *slaughtered to receive power and*
> *wealth and wisdom and might*
> *and honor and glory and blessing!"*

In the next vision I saw the Lamb open one of the seals. As each seal was opened, a scene was shown to me depicting future events upon the earth. After the sixth seal, there came a great earthquake, the sun turned black and the moon like blood. Every mountain and island was moved from its place, and the stars fell from the sky. Every powerful person on earth and everyone, slave and free, hid in caves and among the rocks of the mountain, calling to the rocks, "Fall on us and hide us from the face of the One seated on the throne and from the wrath of the Lamb; for the great day of their wrath has come and who is able to stand?"

And I saw 144,00 having the seal of the living God

on their foreheads; there were 12,000 from each tribe of Israel. And I looked and there was a great multitude that no one could count from every tribe and people and language standing before the throne and before the Lamb.

They were robed in white with palm branches in their hands. And they cried out in a loud voice,

> *"Salvation belongs to our God*
> *who is seated on the*
> *throne and to the Lamb!"*

When I asked one of the elders who these were, he replied,

> *"These are they who have come out of the great ordeal; they have washed their robes and made them white in the blood of the Lamb.*
> *For this reason they are before the throne of God and worship him day and night within his temple. And the One who is seated on the throne will shelter them.*
> *They will hunger and thirst no more; the sun will not strike them, nor any scorching heat;*
> *for the Lamb at the center of the throne will be their shepherd,*
> *and he will guide them to springs of the water of life. And God will wipe away every tear from their eyes."*

After these spectacular visions, I saw the earth controlled by Satan and his beasts and I saw many people give him their allegiance. I viewed plagues and hardships visited upon the unjust and unfaithful of the earth. I witnessed Christ come riding out of heaven on a white horse with the armies of heaven following. I observed Satan's beast and his army defeated, followed by Christ reigning for a thousand years. I saw Satan tossed into the lake of fire with Satan's beasts and the deceiver.

I saw the great white throne of judgment (those who reigned with Christ for 1000 years were excused from this judgment) and all the dead came alive and were judged by what they had done on earth. Anyone whose name was not found in the Book of Life was thrown into the lake of fire.

And I witnessed a new heaven and a new earth, for the old ones had passed away. And I saw God and the Lamb living with mankind in the new earth. And I heard a voice from the throne saying,

> *"See, the home of God is among mortals. He will dwell with them; they will be his people, and God himself will be with them; he will wipe away every tear from their eyes. Death will be no more; mourning and crying and pain will be no more, for the first things have passed away."*

The next morning John again took up the job of recording the visions. He continued adding to the revelation as his recollections cleared. This was a process which would take many more hours to fully complete.

Although his life was not unpleasant, John was lonesome for the companionship of Deborah and his great flock of believers.

XXXIV

Domitian's Fate, John Freed

Meanwhile in Rome, events were transpiring which would have a definite effect on John. The Roman emperor Domitian was becoming more distrustful and neurotic. He continued over-emphasizing his own deification, demanding to be addressed as Master and god. It was John's refusal to make sacrifices to the emperor that had resulted in his exile to Patmos.

Domitian had already put several senators and other officials to death. Now the neurosis turned into a paranoid distrust of his closest associates and friends. When he had his personal secretary put to death as well as his cousin, Flavius Clemens, his own family began to fear him. No one knew who he would turn on next. In this atmosphere, it was not surprising that a plot to assassinate him was hatched. Parthenius, Domitian's chamberlain, with the help of Maximus, a freedman of Parthenius and Stephanus, a steward of

Domitian's niece, planned the assassination. Even Domitian's wife was privy to the plot.

Domitian, already highly disturbed by certain astrological signs, negative predictions, and troubling dreams had imagined that adverse events would occur at a particular time on a certain day. When morning of that day arrived, he arose and anxiously awaited the fateful hour. As the time drew near, he was misled by a servant, who told him that the hour had already passed. Greatly relieved, Domitian started to go to his bath when Parthenius told him someone wanted to see him in his bedroom with a message which could not wait. Domitian found Stephanus waiting, ostensibly with news about a plot to assassinate the emperor. Stephanus had already removed the sword Domitian kept under his pillow, and had hidden a dagger under some bandages on his arm supposedly covering a wound.

When the emperor sat down to read of the conspiracy, Stephanus stabbed him in the groin. Severely wounded, Domitian jumped to his feet in wild eyed astonishment and began to struggle with Stephanus, his bloody fingers gouging out the eyes of his assailant. Several more of the conspirators then entered the room and succeeded in stabbing the emperor to death. His body was carried out on a common bier used for the poor.

The news of the emperor's death was taken with more or less indifference in Rome, but the senate was overjoyed that the dictator was finally put to rest. Their first actions were to strike from all public records any and all mention of Domitian's deeds and accomplishments, to pardon all persons banished, and to restore the properties which had been confiscated. They proclaimed Nerva, an older, distinguished lawyer, to be the new emperor.

It took about three weeks for the news to reach Ephesus, and the Roman officials were happy to send an order to Patmos for the release of John and any other persons sentenced by Domitian. When Gaius reached the cave with the news, John was overcome with joy and God's mercy at the prospect of returning to Ephesus and to all the ones he loved.

Before leaving Patmos, John was invited to dine with the tribune Arrius, who asked the apostle how he could pray for one who had inflicted such pain upon himself and the other prisoners. John immediately sensed that Arrius was seeking help and was open to receiving the gospel. When he revealed the living Christ to the tribune, it was evident that Arrius soaked up every word.

There were many questions and much discussion late into the night. Finally Arrius said, "I would like to accept Christ, but my life is too weighted down with sins and transgressions. The burden has become almost intolerable. I could never be forgiven."

"There is a way," replied John. "It's part of the good news Jesus brought us. The Master has taken away your sins and mine. He has already paid the price. I will account to Christ for your sins if you will confess them."

The next hour involved a scene as strange as any could imagine. The head of the Patmos penal colony laid out his litany of sins in detail to a former prisoner. When he finished, John prayed, "Almighty God, heavenly Father, have mercy on this man. Lift the heavy burden off his shoulders. Forgive all his earnestly confessed sins through the grace and merit of our Lord Jesus Christ. Strengthen him with your Holy Spirit and bring him to eternal life. Amen."

With tears in his eyes, Arrius asked if he could be baptized. Early the next morning before he left the island, John baptized Arrius in the salt water of the Aegean Sea. The apostle had planted many seeds in Patmos, so his time there, while full of hardships, was not wasted and instead turned out to be a blessed evangelistic effort.

When John's ship landed at the harbor of Ephesus, a multitude of Christians from many cities of Asia were there to greet him. Deborah was there also as well as a number of Ephesian officials.

His homecoming was one of the happiest moments of John's life as he walked through the crowd, greeting each person and offering thanks to God.

XXXV

One Last Enemy

After the difficult experience at Patmos, John took several days just to soak up the joy and peace of being with the ones he loved. He was now 89 and he knew that his busy schedule of visiting all the churches in Asia was coming to an end. Also there was much unfinished writing to be done—completing both the gospel and the apocalypse.

However, while he was imprisoned and secluded at Patmos, an ominous development was occurring. Those who had never known Christ were trying to put a different interpretation on the gospel. The euphoria of his freedom was being eclipsed by Cerinthus, a Gnostic heretic who was developing a following. His doctrine basically tried to change the nature of the Creator and the nature of Christ, himself. It involved an indifference to moral values since Gnostics believed the earth and all matter were evil. They advocated access to special knowledge as the means of salvation instead of following Christ. John, being the last of the apostles, felt he had to guard his "little children," his flock in Asia against this and other heresies.

One day John went to the Roman baths in Ephesus with some friends. Cerinthus happened to be in Ephesus also. Upon being told that Cerinthus was in the bath house, John bounced out of the water, quickly dressed and shouted to his friends to get out quickly before the roof caved in. "Cerinthus, the enemy of the truth is inside."

No one else alive had been with Jesus, had experienced the miracles and the grace of Christ. So John wrote a circular letter to the Asian churches. In it he stated, "We declare to you that which we experienced from the beginning, what we heard with our ears and saw with our eyes and even touched with our hands. This life was revealed to us, and we have known it, and we declare to you that this eternal life was with the Father and was revealed to us. That which we have seen and heard we declare to you so that you may have fellowship with us and fellowship with the Father and his Son, Jesus Christ. If we say that we have this fellowship while we are walking in darkness, we lie and are not doing what is true. Walking in the light as he himself walked enables us to have fellowship with one another and the blood of Jesus cleanses us from all sin."

John wrote further, "Who is the liar? It is the one who denies that Jesus is the Christ. The one who denies both the Father and the Son is the antichrist. Those who deny the Son do not have the Father. Conversely, everyone who confesses the Son has the Father also. Abide in what you heard from the beginning. If you do that, you will abide in the Son and in the Father and we are promised eternal life.

"The Father has given us such great love that we can be called children of God. The reason the world does not understand us is that it did not know him. Beloved, we are now God's children but what we will be has not yet been revealed to us. This is what we know: when he is revealed, we will be like him.

"And this is the message we have heard from the beginning: that we should believe in Jesus Christ and love one another. We should not be like Cain who murdered his brother because his own deeds were evil and his brother's deeds were righteous. We are confident that we have passed from death to life because we love one another. The one who does not love abides in death. We know that he expressed his love by laying down his life for us. We should do likewise for each other. Little children, let love be expressed in truth and action and not just in word and speech.

"Beloved, if our hearts do not condemn us, we can be bold before God, asking and receiving that which is according to his will. And he has given us his Spirit as a guarantor of our abiding in him.

"We have seen and testify that God has sent his Son as Savior of the world—to be the atoning sacrifice for our sins. And this is the testimony: God gave us eternal life and this life is in his Son. Therefore, whosoever has the Son has life.

"This is the victory that enables us to conquer the world—our faith."

John believed that this letter would stem the tide of heresies at least until he was able to finish and circulate his gospel.

XXXVI

The Search Finished

Having dealt with the urgent matter of the heresies and feeling confident the bishops were taking care of the Asian churches, John was able to return to his writings. With the help of Deborah, he revisited the apocalypse adding what he now recalled in vivid detail, polishing and crafting the work. He still was able to occasionally visit one of the six churches near Ephesus.

The opening lines of the gospel had not yet been given him, so he waited patiently, attending church services with Deborah and occasionally preaching a sermon, which he could easily do without preparation. When he turned 95, the stamina which he had always been blessed with began to gradually ebb away, and his legs which had carried him on so many journeys began to give out. Finally, he had to be carried into the church on a bier. He would constantly advise, "Little children, love each other as

Christ has loved you, for that is the final commandment the
Lord gave us."

One morning after he had spent most of the night praying,
he summoned Deborah and   saying simply that the Spirit had
moved him, he dictated the missing lines of his gospel:

> *"In the beginning was the Word and the Word*
> *was with God and the Word was God.*
> *He was in the beginning with God.*
> *All things came into being through him,*
> *and without him not one thing came into being.*
> *What has come into being in him was life,*
> *and the life was the light of all people.*
> *The light shines in the darkness,*
> *and the darkness did not overcome it.*
> *There was a man sent from God whose name was*
> *John(the Baptist).*
> *He came as a witness to testify to the light, so that*
> *all might believe through him.*
> *He himself was not the light,*
> *but he came to testify to the light.*
> *The true light which enlightens everyone*
> *was coming into the world.*
> *He was in the world, and the world came into*
> *being through him;*
> *yet the world did not know him.*
> *He came to what was his own,*
> *and his own people did not accept him.*
> *But to all who received him, who believed in his*
> *name, he gave power to become children of God,*
> *who were born not of blood or of the will of the*
> *flesh or of the will of man, but of God.*
> *And the Word became flesh and lived among us,*

and we have seen his glory, the glory as of a
father's only son, full of grace and truth.
(John testified to him and cried out, 'This was he
of whom I said,
"He who comes after me ranks ahead of me
because he was before me."')
From his fullness we have all received grace
upon grace.
The law indeed was given through Moses,
grace and truth came through Jesus Christ.
No one has ever seen God.
It is God the only Son who is close to the Father's
heart, who has made him known."

When he had concluded the dictation, John took Deborah's hand, looked into her eyes and faintly said, "I have finished my search. My gospel is complete. The church will reveal it to the world. When called, I can now go in peace."

High above Ephesus an eagle soared into the sky.

SCRIPTURE QUOTATIONS
List of quoted Old and New Testament passages

Luke 3:4-6 NRSV p.11
Matt. 3:7b-10 NRSV p.12
Luke 3:4-6 NRSV p.21
Isaiah 53:6 p.21
Matt. 3:11-12 NRSV p.21
Amos 5:21-24 NRSV p.33
Isaiah 58:3b-9 NRSV p.33
Isaiah 9:1-6 NRSV p.37
Isaiah 11:1-4 NRSV p.38
Isaiah 42:1 AB p.38
Isaiah 49:6 AB p.38
John 2:17 NRSV p.53
John 3:16,17 NRSV p.58
Mark 1:15 NRSV p.63
Isaiah 9:2 NIV p.63
Dan. 7:13-14 KJV p.66
Deut. 8:3 p.67
Matt. 4:10b, Deut. 6:13 p.67
Deut. 6:16 NRSV p.67
John 6:53-58 NIV p.75
John 6:61b-63 NRSV p.76

John 10:11-18 NIV p.87
Zech. 9:9 NRSV p.93
John 14:5,6 NIV p.95
Zech. 13:7 NIV p.99
Isaiah 50: 6b KJV p.102
Deut. 21:23b NRSV p.102
Isaiah 52:14 NRSV p.104
Psalm 22:18 NRSV p. 108
Psalm 34:20 NIV p.110
Zech. 12:10 p.110
Isaiah 53:4,5,6b,8,10b,11 NRSV p
Acts 4:11 p.124, Ps. 118:22
Acts 4:25,26 NRSV p.125, Ps. 2:1
Isaiah 40:31 NRSV p.157
Matt. 5:44 NRSV p.158
Rev. 4:11 NRSV p.164
Rev. 5: 9-10 NRSV p.165
Rev. 5:12 NRSV p.165
Rev. 7:10 NRSV p. 166
Rev. 7:14b-17 NRSV p.166
Rev. 21:3b-4 NRSV p.167
John 1:1-18 NRSV p.178

Author's note: Where quotations are verbatim, the translation is indicated. Where one
more words are different, no version is indicated.

Study Questions

Chapter I

1. Describe the difference between the Province of Judah and Galilee in the 1st Century.
2. What is your concept of the Jewish path of salvation.
3. How would you characterize John, his personality, his outlook on life?

Chapter II

1. How would you describe the Province of Samaria in the 1st Century.
2. Discuss the fishing business of Zebedee.
3. How did one of John's business duties lead to his experiencing the desert preacher?

Chapter III

1. Give your description of John the Baptist.
2. How would you characterize his basic message"
3. What did he mean by "the ax is now at the root of the tree"?
4. What practical immediate action did he recommend to the people?

Chapter IV

1. If you were approaching Jerusalem on the Jericho road, how would you describe the city?
2. What kept John so long at the palace of the high priest?

Chapter V

1. Explain Zebedee's attitude toward the Prophet.
2. What were the new words of the Prophet which John had not heard before?

Chapter VI

1. How would you describe Andrew?
2. Have you ever felt an overwhelming desire to follow your yearnings even when they conflicted with family, friends?
3. Have you found the truth—the ultimate meaning of life, your connection with the Creator, your true calling in life, your real significance as a human being?

Chapter VII

1. Why did John and Andrew follow the Prophet?
2. What made it a difficult decision for the Baptist to accept the young men?
3. Describe the food eaten by the Prophet. Would you have relished it as John and Andrew did?

Chapter VIII

1. Describe a typical day for the young men as they learned from the Prophet.
2. What did the Baptist compare John to? Why?
3. Discuss the early life of the Baptist and how it led him to the wilderness preaching and baptisms?

4. Besides the severe warnings, what other aspects of the prophets did the Baptist emphasize?

Chapter IX

1. What subject did the Baptist stay away from during the first few weeks?
2. Which prophet did the Baptist start quoting concerning the coming Messiah?
3. Did the Baptist know who the Messiah was?

Chapter X

1. What did the delegation from the Council in Jerusalem want?
2. At what moment did the Baptist and the crowd really notice Jesus? If you had been in the crown, what would have been your reaction?
3. Describe the Baptist's feelings when the young disciples decided to follow Jesus.

Chapter XI

1. Why do you think Jesus went to Galilee the day after John and Andrew joined him?
2. Name the next four disciples after John and James. Of the first six disciples, how many were fishermen?
3. When Jesus called the four fishermen, John and James, Peter and Andrew, what did he say he would make them? Have you ever had a similar call?

Chapter XII

1. When did John first experience the miraculous power of Jesus?
2. When Jesus began his public ministry and many began to come to him, what three things did he do or emphasize?

3. When John visited Deborah again, what ominous warning did she reveal? What event gave John serious worries about the Jewish authorities?

Chapter XIII

1. Jesus had two significant discussions with what two unusual people?
2. What did Jesus tell the teacher of the Jews was necessary for salvation? Have you experienced this same thing?
3. When Jesus and the disciples started back to Galilee, what route did he choose? Explain the reason for Jesus taking this route.

Chapter XIV

1. According to Scripture, what were the first words Jesus emphasized as he taught the people?
2. Describe the father in the Prodigal Son parable. Who was Jesus describing?
3. Name at least two teachings of Jesus which "fulfilled" the law and the prophets.
4. What happened to Jesus after the Spirit drove him into the wilderness? Have you ever experienced the call or direction of the Spirit in your life?

Chapter XV

1. What important principle did Jesus reveal in healing the child of the Capernaum royal official?
2. What did the crippled man Jesus healed say to the Pharisees which caused them to condemn Jesus?
3. What made Deborah hurry by night to tell John?
4. In what geographical area was the ministry of Jesus unimpeded by the Jewish authorities?

Chapter XVI

1. Describe how Jesus introduced the truth that he was the "bread of life?"
2. Jesus taught the Jews that they must eat his body and drink his blood if they were to be saved for eternal life. Why did the Jews find this teaching so hard to believe?
3. What two future events did this teaching point to?
4. How did Jesus compare the spirit and the flesh? Can you relate to this?

Chapter XVII

1. What were the Jews arguing about which caused the chief priests to send temple police to arrest Jesus ?
2. What straight forward truth did Jesus reveal to the disciples? If you had been one of the disciples, how would you have received this revelation?
3. Describe Zebedee's change of heart. What brought it on?

Chapter XVIII

1. What did Zebedee ask Jesus to do? How did Salome react to John's experience with Jesus?
2. Why did the Jewish authorities not arrest Jesus as he taught openly in the temple?
3. What was Jesus' reaction to the woman caught in adultery? Where was the man? Do you think this whole situation was a plot to undermine Jesus? What do you think Jesus wrote in the sand?
4. Explain the attitude and reaction of the Pharisees to the healing of the man born blind.
5. How did the Pharisees react to the statements of the man born blind?

Chapter XIX

1. Explain the metaphor of the good shepherd and how it applied to Jesus.
2. Who was Jesus speaking of when he said there were "other flocks" and he must also bring them in?
3. Why did King Herod arrest John the Baptist and have him executed?
4. Describe the mountain top event John experienced with Jesus. What would have been your reaction?
5. What effect did the raising of Lazarus have on the Jews from Jerusalem?
6. What prophesy did Caiaphas unknowingly make about Jesus?

Chapter XX

1. Describe Jesus' entry into Jerusalem.
2. What two most important actions did Jesus take at the last supper?
3. What was the answer of Jesus to Thomas' question about the way to the place Jesus was going?
4. Explain what took place in Judas to cause him to betray Jesus. What was his rationalization?
5. Explain the metaphor of the vine. Can you personalize this metaphor?
6. Why did the Jewish authorities want to arrest Jesus at night?

Chapter XXI

1. Imagine you were present at the midnight trial of Jesus. Describe what took place.
2. How many times did Peter deny knowing Jesus?
3. Why do you think the Jewish council wanted Jesus to be executed by the Romans?
4. Describe Pilate's attitude. Why did he give in to the Jews?

Chapter XXII

1. Describe the Roman version of crucifixion. Why had they adopted such an inhuman method of execution?
2. Explain the significance of Jesus' remark to the repentant and respectful thief.
3. For what reason did the Jews want the bodies removed from the cross so that they broke the legs of the two bandits to hasten death? How did they make sure Jesus was dead?
4. Why do you think Jesus give his mother to John rather than have her stay in Nazareth with her family?
5. Who asked for the body of Jesus? For what reason?
6. On the first day of the week Mary Magdalene found the stone rolled away. Who did she report this to? Who was the first disciple to believe Jesus was resurrected from the dead? Who was the first to actually see Jesus after his resurrection?

Chapter XXIII

1. Describe the first and second meetings of Jesus with the disciples in the upper room. Pretend you are Thomas and you missed the first meeting. What would have been your attitude?
2. While taking a rest in Galilee and an all night fishing trip, how did John recognize the man on the shore as Jesus?
3. Explain how Jesus forgave Peter for his three denials.
4. Can you recall the prophesies Jesus made concerning Peter and John?

Chapter XXIV

1. Name the happy and the sad news about Zebedee.
2. Trace John's meditation about the reason Jesus had to die and be resurrected. Elaborate on your own beliefs in this regard.
3. Describe the experience of the Apostle's receiving the Holy Spirit.

4. What extraordinary events followed the coming of the Spirit?
5. Explain how the last commandment of the Lord about love began to really come alive?

Chapter XXV

1. When the disciples were brought before the Jewish authorities, what were they forbidden to do? How would you have reacted? Peter made one of his inspired speeches. Explain the metaphor of the stone.
2. What happened to the special prosecutor appointed by the chief priests to wipe out the Christian movement?
3. Explain the vision Peter had on the house top and how it affected his thinking about Gentiles.

Chapter XXVI

1. How did Peter avoid James' fate?
2. What happened to King Herod?

Chapter XXVII

1. How did the Gospel get carried to Ethiopia?
2. What introspection did John experience at this point in his life? Have you ever had a similar experience?
3. Describe what happened in Antioch of Syria.
4. There was a strong physical attraction between John and Deborah. What kept John from marrying her?
5. What made the church at Antioch so very special?
6. What exceptional insight did Peter and John have about the Christian mission?

Chapter XXVIII

1. As the Apostles made preparation to leave Jerusalem for the "ends of he earth," what immense event took place?
2. Some Apostles were sent away as far as Spain. Where did Peter and John go?
3. Who had prepared the way for John in Ephesus? This first Christian mission in Ephesus left two highly motivated Christians there. Who were they, and how did they receive John?
4. Describe how John saved Jason.
5. After several years of building up the church in Asia, what bad news did John receive? What did this prompt John to do?

Chapter XXIX

1. Imagine you are John returning to Jerusalem. Describe what you would have seen?
2. Not finding the body of his mother in the Malachi house, what kept John from looking for Deborah at the high priest's palace?
3. Recall the prophecy of Jesus concerning Jerusalem.
4. Where did John go after leaving Jerusalem? Who did he find there"
5. Recall the words of Jesus to the Samaritan woman concerning worship.

Chapter XXX

1. Back in Ephesus John asked Deborah to marry him. What was her reply? Explain.

Chapter XXXI

1. What was John's new calling? How was this confirmed?
2. After two years of writing, John had almost a complete manuscript. What was missing?
3. Why was John sentenced to the penal colony at Patmos?

Chapter XXXII

1. Describe the conditions at the Patmos penal colony. Could you have survived this experience?
2. What name did John acquire at Patmos? Why?
3. What was John called upon to do which he found to be difficult? In similar circumstances, could you do the same?
4. In what ways did the Tribune show his appreciation to John?

Chapter XXXIII

1. What happened to John when he went for a walk on the first day of the week?
2. Describe at least one scene in John's vision.
3. What was John told to do concerning the visions?

Chapter XXXIV

1. Explain Emperor Domitian's state of mind toward the end of his reign.
2. Why was a plot hatched to kill Domitian?
3. What actions did the Roman senate take after the emperor's death? The Roman officials at Ephesus?
4. What was so hard for Arrius, the Roman tribune at Patmos, to understand.
5. Discuss the change in Arrius, his redemption.

Chapter XXXV

1. What was the last enemy John faced?
2. What did John do to win this last battle?
3. Name some of the themes in John's letter.

Chapter XXXVI

1. Why had John not found the opening verses to his gospel?
2. Explain the end of John's search.

R. C. Balfour, III graduated Phi Beta Kappa from the University of Georgia with a degree in Political Science. His business career was spent in land management and lumber manufacturing with a strong emphasis on environmental stewardship. He served the Diocese of Georgia as chairman of the Evangelism and Stewardship Commission, and was later elected deputy to the General Convention of the Episcopal Church. He served his community as a City Commissioner and later as Chairman of the Board of Archbold Medical Center. His first two books, *In Search of the Aucilla* and *Fishing for the Abundant Life* were published in 2002 and 2003. These were followed by *He Turned the World Upside Down* in 2007 and *Paul Speaks to Us Today* in 2011. He is married to the former Virginia French, and they are the proud parents of three boys and two girls and grandparents of eight.